UNSHAKEABLE

STORIES TO ANCHOR YOU THROUGH LIFE'S STORMS

CAREY CONLEY

Published by Cloversy LLC DBA Cloversy Publishing. (480) 910-4111. www.Cloversy.com.

DISCLAIMER AND/OR LEGAL NOTICES

While all attempts have been made to verify the information provided in this book and its ancillary materials, neither the author nor the publisher assume any responsibility for errors, inaccuracies, or omissions and are not responsible for any financial loss by the customer in any manner. Any slights of people or organizations are unintentional. If advice concerning legal, financial, accounting, or related matters is needed, the services of a qualified professional should be sought. This book and its associated ancillary materials, including verbal and written training, is not intended for use as a source of legal, financial, or accounting advice. You should be aware of the various laws governing business transactions or other business practices in your particular geographical location.

EARNINGS & INCOME DISCLAIMER

With respect to the reliability, accuracy, timeliness, usefulness, adequacy, completeness, and/ or suitability of the information provided in this book, Cloversy, LLC. make no warranties, guarantees, representations, or claims of any kind. Readers' results will vary depending on a number of factors. Any and all claims or representations as to income earnings are not to be considered as average earnings. Testimonials are not representative. This book and all products and services are for educational and informational purposes only. Use caution and seek the advice of qualified professionals. Check with your accountant, attorney, or professional advisor before acting on this or any information. Earnings potential is entirely dependent on the efforts, skills, and application of the individual person.

Any examples, stories, reference, or case studies are for illustrative purposes only and should not be interpreted as testimonies and/or examples of what reader and/ or consumers can generally expect from the information. Any statements, strategies, concepts, techniques, exercises, and ideas in the information and materials offered are simply opinion or experience, and thus should not be misinterpreted as promises, typical results, or guarantees (expressed or implied). This book is provided "as is" and without warranties.

ISBN: 978-0-9966999-4-5

Printed in the United States of America

Table of Contents

Introduction

We all endure storms of varying intensity throughout our lives, and the anchors we lower to stabilize ourselves look different from person to person. My hope is that one or more of these stories will resonate with you as you drop your own anchor and navigate your journey.

I curated this collection of stories to share unique perspectives, in addition to my own. Each of these amazing authors shares encouragement, hope, and resources for those who may be going through similar challenges. My genuine hope is that these inspiring stories will help you discover anchors to apply to your own situation.

This book is not only for you, but also for you to share with others who could use it as a resource to help them through hard times. No matter what you or your loved ones are dealing with, these chapters are here to help you.

Above all, through reading the stories in this book, I hope you take away the most important message of all: you are not alone.

Carey Conley

Foreword

Life has a way of bringing us to our knees.

No matter how successful we become, how carefully we plan our future, or how much we feel we are in control—we all face storms that shake us to our core. I know this intimately. After building global brands, writing New York Times Bestselling books, advising U.S. presidents, and championing financial literacy around the globe, nothing could have prepared me for the heartbreak of losing my son in 2012. In that moment, every accomplishment and every accolade vanished. The world moved on, but I was left numb, standing still, living my life in neutral and questioning how to move forward when the ground beneath me had given way.

I was so lost that I almost retired back in 2014, but I received a lot of pushback from family and friends. And even heard my son in my ear saying, "Mom you are still here for a reason, you have more to do! Get busy!" I took that message to heart, and focused my energy on helping others navigate their storms to find their definite purpose in life.

I am honored to write the foreword for this powerful collection of people's stories of heartfelt perseverance and healing because I believe in its mission. We don't heal by pretending we're okay. We heal by telling the truth, finding connection in our brokenness, and reminding each other that we are never truly alone in the storm.

Each story is shared by real people who have weathered life's fiercest storms—not with perfection, but with courage. And through sharing their pain, they offer us something far greater than comfort. They offer us anchors—wisdom, perspective, and hope we can hold onto when everything else feels uncertain.

You may find a story that mirrors your own storm, or others that share advice and wisdom that will help you define your own definite purpose in life.

That's why Unshakeable is more than just a book—it's a testament to the resilience of the human spirit.

To every reader holding this book: may these pages meet you exactly where you are. And may they remind you that even in the fiercest winds, you are not powerless. You are unshakeable.

From my heart to yours,

Sharon Lechter
5X New York Times Bestselling Author, Keynote Speaker and Business Master Mentor
Author of Think and Grow Rich for Women, Co-author of Rich Dad Poor Dad and 14 other books in the Rich Dad series, Three Feet From Gold, Outwitting the Devil, Exit Rich and How Money Works for Women
www.sharonlechter.com

Three Generations of Orchids

By Alice Chen

The orchid has always been the quiet emblem of my family. Elegant. Resilient. Refined. With a beauty that's not loud, but lingers. Orchids thrive in conditions that would wilt other blooms. They survive in the shadows, drawing strength from stillness, blooming not for applause—but because it is their nature.

My grandmother, Waipo, was like that.

Like her, I was born on the island of Taiwan, a land shaped by sea and struggle, colonized by the Dutch, then the Japanese. It was there that my ancestors—descendants of both the Han Chinese and Taiwan's Indigenous "Hill's People"—endured generations of upheaval and learned to carry on with quiet strength.

My maternal grandparents were raised during Japanese rule. My grandfather was one of the few non-Japanese to graduate from their school system—junior high, then high school, then a technical institute. Eventually, he became one of the engineers who helped build Taiwan's railway system. He was disciplined, rational, principled, and deeply shaped by a world of hierarchy and order.

My grandmother lived in his shadow.

She didn't get to go to school. That wasn't for girls. Her role was dictated by tradition: she served her husband, raised children, and ran the household. Every Saturday of my childhood, we'd visit their home, and I would observe the intricate dance of duty. Waipo shopped for fresh seafood, stewed soup, and laid out clothes for my grandfather with quiet precision. He would return home, nod, and say, "Shatsu. Pantsu." Shirts. Pants. She would lay them out without a word. It was understood.

In the early years, I watched her sew dolls while the men discussed politics and the women cleared the table. She stitched them with such concentration, almost meditation. I asked my mother why. She told me Waipo sold the dolls to make some money now that her children were grown.

Years passed. The dolls disappeared. And then I saw her writing Chinese characters in a notebook. She was learning to read and write.

"She's in grade four," my mom said, smiling. "Same as you."

At sixty-four, my grandmother was back in school. She graduated elementary school as valedictorian. Then she enrolled in senior's university. At seventy, she graduated again.

All the while, she continued preparing those Saturday feasts. Continued laying out her husband's clothes. Continued being the anchor of our family.

But something changed.

Her glow deepened. Her presence softened and strengthened at once. A calm power radiated from her—an orchid, fully in bloom.

There's a Chinese proverb that says: "*The orchid grows where others cannot thrive. It does not shout, yet fills the room with fragrance.*"

That was my grandmother.

She didn't rise through revolt. She didn't reject her traditions. Instead, she chose to root deeper in her own truth—and slowly, intentionally, transform.

Her power wasn't in how loudly she spoke—but in how clearly she knew who she was becoming

I didn't know it then, but Waipo's quiet bloom would become my compass. Her strength flowed through my mother, too—a woman who trail-blazed as one of Taiwan's first female bankers while being a dutiful wife and attentive mother of three. I inherited their grit, their vision, and their discipline.

Years later, I would need to remember this.

I had graduated from law school and earned a seat at the most prestigious corporate law firm in Canada—without legacy connections, alumni networks, or an insider's map. Just grit, instinct, and relentless effort. After that, I went on to build businesses in international trade, finance and investments, consumer goods, and technology.

Every time I wanted access—whether to a boardroom, an industry, or an opportunity—I didn't have the VIP pass. So I found the back door, broke through the fence, and somehow got myself to the front row.

On the surface, I became someone people respected. I was well-networked. Thriving. But underneath, I was running on fumes.

I was constantly trying to outwork people who had more capital, more connections, and fewer limitations. I was still playing their game—just with more elegant armor. Deep down, I knew: this wasn't the life I came here to build.

I felt trapped inside a game I hadn't designed—and knew I couldn't win by their rules. Then I thought of Waipo. I thought of her notebooks. Her quiet resolve. And I asked myself: *What if I stopped trying to win their game—and start creating my own?*

Each time, I flipped the script of an incumbent industry and emerged as a formidable disruptor and challenger. My ability for deep strategy and innovation is now widely respected. Just like Waipo and her quiet decision to bloom, not through rebellion, but through choosing herself.

I wasn't just changing my business models. I was changing my identity. I stopped asking, *How do I compete?* and began asking, *What am I here to create?*

Today, I help others realize: you are not bound by who you have been. You are only bound by the stories you continue to believe.

The truth is, identity is not fixed. It's chosen. And it can be changed at any moment. Not with struggle, or striving—but with one simple act: A decision.

The orchid reminds us of this. In both Chinese and Japanese cultures, the orchid symbolizes elegance, purity, and rare inner strength. Orchids are slow bloomers. They may take years to flower. But when they do, they're unmatched in their grace and refinement.

They require care, yes—but they also require courage.

Courage to bloom in silence.
Courage to grow where no one thought you could.
Courage to redefine what power looks like.

That is the legacy of my grandmother. That is what I now carry into every room I enter—not just as an investor, or a speaker, or a founder—but as a woman who knows: *I can choose who I am becoming, at any time.*

My grandmother is now gone, but she left me everything I need. Not through words—but by example. She showed me that storms may shake the surface, but they do not define who we are. We define that. Every moment. With every choice.

You Are the Orchid.

So here is your invitation:

You don't need to be loud to be powerful.
You don't need to wait to be chosen.
You don't need permission to become someone new.

You are the orchid.

You can bloom slowly.
You can bloom differently.
But you *will* bloom—when you decide it's time.

What if this moment . . . is your moment?

It takes just one choice. And once you choose—it is done.

Today, I work with legacy industries that many consider slow to evolve—real estate, land development, private equity. On the surface, these fields don't seem to have anything in common with a story about my grandmother. But in reality they do. Because just like her, these industries have long followed rigid rules. Just like her, new entrants into these industries are often underestimated. And just like her, they are capable of radical reinvention—when guided with care, vision, and courage.

Through my platform, LegacyLift, I help founders, developers, and capital managers unlock new forms of power by integrating AI systems, modern workflows, and more intuitive business models. It's not just about technology—it's about transformation. It's about shedding inherited constraints and designing from first principles. In many ways, I help others do what I had to learn for myself: to stop trying to fit into systems that weren't built for us, and instead build systems that reflect who we truly are becoming.

This is the essence of what I now call the Orchid Framework: a process of identity-led innovation. It honors tradition, but doesn't get trapped by it. It invites grace into growth, and reminds us that reinvention doesn't require rebellion—it requires clarity, conviction, and a willingness to choose again.

My grandmother never set foot in a boardroom, but she taught me everything I needed to know about power. Real power is not about volume or velocity—it's about presence. It's about blooming fully, wherever you are.

Whether you're scaling a company, reinventing a career, or simply trying to hear your own voice again—remember this: You are the orchid. You are allowed to be both strong and soft, rooted and visionary. And when you choose to bloom, nothing can stop you.

And if you ever feel like you've hit a wall—when the path forward seems unclear—remember, you don't have to do it alone. Look back. There are always those who came before you, quietly blazing trails with grace and grit. Let their stories remind you of what's possible. Let their courage become your compass.

Remember:

"You are the orchid. You can bloom slowly. You can bloom differently. But you will bloom—when you decide it's time."

"You can honor your past without living inside its limits."

"Legacy isn't what you inherit. It's what you choose to carry forward.

About the Author

Alice Chen is a lawyer-turned-entrepreneur and investor who has built and exited businesses across international trade, finance, consumer goods, and technology. Drawing inspiration from her grandmother's resilience, Alice empowers others to transform their identities and embrace their true selves in life, business and mission.

"You are the orchid. You can bloom slowly.
You can bloom differently.
But you will bloom—when you decide it's time."

Scan the QR Code to Learn More

Ready to Bloom Into Who You're Meant to Become?

If something in my story stirred something in you—an identity you're ready to outgrow, or a calling you're finally ready to claim—this is your invitation.

Doing Hard Things

By Ben Anderson

We humans are born to tell stories. From ancient tribes sharing tales of triumph and struggle around flickering campfires to Navajo and Aboriginal peoples weaving wisdom through oral histories, storytelling is in our blood. It's how we make sense of life's chaos, how we inspire each other. The printing press carried those stories from small fires to the wider world, but their heart remains the same: they guide us, like lighthouses in a storm, with examples of grit and courage. As Alex Hormozi once said, "The bigger the monster, the greater the hero. Whatever trials you're facing, they'll become the stories you tell." My monster arrived one Sunday morning, when a phone call upended my world and threw me into the fiercest storm I'd ever faced.

I was twenty-six, a husband, a dad to two girls under two. Beth, my wife, had been under the weather for days—fevers coming and going, her breathing growing labored. Around 3 a.m., she asked me to take her to the ER. I'll be honest: I was a little annoyed, thinking she might be overreacting, already stressing about the hospital bill and our two babies at home. But I drove her, dropped her off, and went back to crash, figuring I'd sort it out later.

It wasn't my 18-month-old's chatter or the stirrings of our 3-month-old in her bassinet that woke me five hours later. It was my phone buzzing with "Unknown Caller." I ignored it, muttering about spam calls at 8 a.m. on a Sunday. Then the voicemail came: "Mr. Anderson, this is Dr. Thompson. I'm treating your wife, Beth. Mr. Anderson, we need you to come to the ICU. It's about your wife. We need you to make decisions about her life. Please hurry."

Those words hit like a freight train. My world tilted. Our small family was living with Beth's parents at the time, so I mumbled something to her dad about the call, left the girls with them, and sped to the hospital, my mind spiraling. *What's happening? I just dropped her off a few hours ago.*

At the hospital, I checked in, barely holding it together. The doctor came out, calm but direct, and laid out my new reality. Beth had severe pneumonia that had turned septic, her lungs filling with fluid. They'd placed her in a medically-induced coma to stabilize her and were pumping her with IV meds. He walked me through treatment options, tests, procedures, then dropped the bomb: "Mr. Anderson, when I have patients presenting in her condition, they have about a 50/50 chance of survival."

A coin toss. My wife's life, reduced to the same odds as picking heads or tails. It felt like some cruel cosmic game, except the stakes were eternal. Despair hit me hard. Tears streamed down my face, and I couldn't stop them. The doctor's last few words blurred as my world crumbled.

He pulled me back, guiding me through decisions—tests to run, treatments to approve. He asked about Beth's medical history, and I almost laughed. "Doc, you got a few hours?" I said, trying to lighten the weight. Beth's health was never simple; her chart could fill a novel.

When we finished, I asked for a moment alone. I sat there in the waiting room, as my head spun. *What do I tell her parents? Our girls? What should I do?* I felt utterly helpless, trapped in a storm I couldn't control. So, I did the only thing I could think of—I prayed. Not some rote prayer—I poured my heart out, begging, bargaining, pleading with God. At that moment, a familiar phrase echoed in my mind, one I'd shared with others—This isn't your first rodeo.

Memories flooded back—hard times I'd faced, challenges I'd overcome. Some I'd brought on myself; others, like this, just happened. They reminded me that I'd done hard things before. A quiet calm settled over me, a steady assurance that I could face this too.

Viktor Frankl once wrote, "When we are no longer able to change a situation, we are challenged to change ourselves." I couldn't fix Beth's illness, but I could change me. I steadied my emotions, called family with what little I knew, and started making decisions that would shape the weeks ahead. I went from lost and helpless to tackling each problem, weighing options, and taking the next right step.

Stepping into that hospital room, I wasn't ready for the sight of Beth hooked to a breathing machine, wires and tubes crisscrossing her body. The weight of it hit like a wave, but I watched the doctors and nurses move with quiet, determined focus. Over the next few days, hope flickered—Beth's fever broke first. I watched as the doctor drained fluid from her lungs. Eventually, the infection began to retreat. After five days, they gently brought her out of the coma. By the end of the next week, she was home, healing, and we were together again, stronger for it.

Back then, I didn't see how past struggles had prepared me for that fight. Those lessons, buried deep, rushed back when I needed them—showing me what worked, where I'd stumbled, how to keep going. This wasn't just another hurdle; it was *the* hurdle, built on every one before it. It wouldn't be the last, but it taught me to see life's challenges as stepping stones, shaping who I'm meant to be.

Fourteen years later, I found myself in another hospital waiting room. This time, Beth was having open-heart surgery. We knew it was coming and prepared the best we could, but it didn't make it easier. I didn't leave her alone in an ER that time. I spent the morning with her, cherishing every moment—telling her I love her, how proud I am, reminding her we've faced hard things before. Joseph Campbell wrote, "The cave you fear to enter holds the treasure you seek." This surgery was another cave, but we'd found light in those dark and daunting caves before. Beth's courage, my resolve—they were our beacons of bravery, steadying us for the fight through the dark ahead.

Sitting there, alone and waiting, doubts crept in. *What if this doesn't go well? What do I tell our girls? Was that the last time I'll see her?* When those thoughts hit, I leaned on the past. We'd faced tough stuff—together and apart—and we'd come through. I'd done hard things before, and I could do them again.

I know you've faced hard things, too. You may not see it yet, but your challenges have prepared you for the mountains ahead. They don't always feel monumental in the moment—sometimes they're just "life"—but they're stepping stones, shaping who you're becoming.

As a coach, I find joy in helping others recognize this truth. I love reminding people: you've tackled hard things before, you can do it again, and more will come. But you'll get through. One of my favorite quotes says it best: "The hardest thing you've done is the hardest thing you've done." Your struggles aren't mine, and mine aren't yours. It's not a competition—there's no prize for suffering the most. We each face unique challenges, and we overcome them, sometimes alone, sometimes with help.

And Beth? She came through the surgery, better than we'd dared hope, but recovery hasn't been easy. She's battling fluid in her lungs—an eerie echo of fourteen years ago—along with muscle cramps, a 10-inch scar down her chest, sleepless nights, and medication challenges. Beth's my hero, facing more than I can fathom. My "hard things" feel small next to hers, but we're getting through it together, another challenge conquered, and we're stronger for it.

As a coach, I'm passionate about helping others uncover their own stories and see they've triumphed, too. Your story holds power—it shapes who you are. Grab a notebook or talk to someone you trust; share one challenge you've overcome. I'm here to help you tell it. Life isn't about who's suffered most. It's about foundations, each challenge grounding you and building you up, helping you to do the next right thing. You've overcome before, and you'll do it again.

About the Author:

With over 20 years of leadership experience, Ben Anderson specializes in coaching high performers and leaders to unlock their full potential. Given his life's journey and struggle with obesity, his focus also includes guiding bariatric surgery patients toward sustainable, high-performance lifestyles, empowering them to achieve a better life. Through personalized strategies, Ben works to inspire growth, resilience, and success, helping clients excel in their personal and professional journeys while fostering lasting transformation and fulfillment.

Scan the QR Code to Learn More

You read how I overcame some of my own hard things – but now it is your turn! Reach out through the link below and schedule a quick 30-mins free coaching session to discuss your own hard things and how to overcome them.

"And Then What?": From Total Collapse to Great Rebirth

By Brandon Hintz

"Sometimes the only way forward is through the wreckage. God doesn't waste pain. He repurposes it."

You were born to do something great with your life. Not just success on paper. Purpose. Impact. Growth. And sometimes, that greatness isn't found in the spotlight. Sometimes it's found in the shadows. In the moments when everything falls apart, and you have to fight like hell just to keep going.

This chapter isn't about what I lost. It's about what I discovered.

The man I was became the man I am because of the storm. What you're about to read is more than a story. It's a reminder that adversity doesn't come to define you. It comes to reveal you.

Everything in life is temporary. The pain. The loss. The silence. The pressure. All of it. But most people never get to the other side of the trial because they quit too early. They never meet the next version of themselves.

I almost didn't either.

There are moments in life when the storm doesn't just hit. It shreds everything to pieces.

I remember gripping the steering wheel of my silver truck like it was the last thing tethering me to reality. I'd driven the same road every day for the last three months, always with the same routine: Xanax in the console, vodka tucked into the passenger-side door, and Vicodin waiting for me at night. But that day felt different. The sky was dull, the air thick with smoke from nearby fires. It was the kind of morning that looked like the world was giving up.

And I knew, deep in my soul, that I couldn't keep living like this. It was going to kill me...

The mortgage industry had collapsed. Everything I had worked for . . . the buildings, the teams, the reputation . . . was dissolving before my eyes. Just months earlier, I had a thriving company, multi-state offices, and a future expanding into banking. Then came 2008. The economy imploded. The Lehman Brothers bankruptcy, followed by a number of major mortgage lenders imploding day by day. There was even a website tracking each one as they filed for bankruptcy.

Clients vanished. Lenders pulled out. Accounts froze. Overnight, I went from leader to survivalist. From empire builder to burnout.

But worse than the absence of money was the silence. The phones stopped ringing. The buzz disappeared. And the pressure of pretending like I had it all under control pushed me further into the pills and booze just to feel okay enough to walk into my own office . . . or even to go home to my family.

I was unraveling. I was self-medicating the stress, and I didn't know how to stop it.

Until the day I sat down with my mentor, Jeff.

He leaned across his desk with that no-nonsense look in his eyes and asked, "What are you going to do next?"

I stared at him. Blank. "I don't know. Everything's falling apart. I've got employees depending on me. Leases. Equipment. There's nothing left to do."

He nodded calmly. "And then what?"

I squinted. "What?"

Jeff didn't flinch. "And then what?"

I shifted in my seat, starting to get irritated. "I'll probably have to start firing people. Shut down branches. Try to keep the collectors off my back."

"And then what?" he said again.

This went on for three rounds. Me offering a bunch of pain each time, and excuses . . . .

My chest tightened. "Jeff, if you say 'and then what' one more time, I swear I'm coming across this desk."

He smiled and leaned back. "Exactly. You can't control any of that. It's out of your hands. So stop trying to control the uncontrollable. Keep what you can. Regroup. Control what's yours. Let the rest go."

His words hit me like a freight train. For weeks, I'd been trying to fight gravity. But Jeff was right. I was drowning because I was holding onto everything. Especially what I couldn't fix.

That night, I couldn't sleep. I sat up, staring at the ceiling, the faint smell of alcohol still clinging to my breath. I kept hearing his words.

"*This too shall pass*!" came to mind.

Then it rang out . . . the Serenity Prayer:

God, grant me the serenity to accept the things I cannot change, Courage to change the things I can, And the wisdom to know the difference.

That next morning, I got into the car like usual. The air was sharp, cool but humid. I could smell the asphalt warming beneath my tires. Same drive. Same pain. But something stirred inside me this time. A whisper I hadn't heard in months: This is not *you*. You don't need this crutch.

I glanced at the pill bottle resting in the center console. I reached for it, paused, then rolled down the window and chucked it out onto the shoulder.

Instant regret. What if a kid finds that?

I took the next turn, circled back, found the bottle in the dirt, cracked it open, and filled it with water from a half-empty bottle in my seat. I shook it until everything inside turned to liquid. I poured it down the gutter, watching the poison swirl away.

I exhaled like I hadn't in months. And for the first time in what felt like forever, I felt clean.

When I walked into the office that day, I already knew what I needed to do.

The place was eerily quiet. Fluorescent lights flickered above rows of half-filled cubicles. Coffee cups left behind. Whiteboards still scribbled with pipeline goals we'd never reach. I stood in the center of the main branch. The one I'd once dreamed of expanding into a bank. And I shouted,

"It's my *time*! My time is *now*!"

It echoed off the glass walls like a battle cry.

That afternoon, I made the call. We were closing every branch except one. But before we did, I gathered everyone in the main building.

There were more than eighty people standing shoulder to shoulder, staring at me with uncertainty written across their faces. Some were angry. Some scared. Some just numb. I stood in front of them and gave the most honest speech I'd ever delivered.

I said, "I'm not asking you to stay. I'm not even asking you to believe in this industry anymore. What I am offering is an invitation. To twenty of you. You're being asked to come with me into the unknown. The market's a mess. The future's unclear. But I believe that this isn't the last chapter. This is the one we get to write."

You could hear a pin drop.

I looked around the room and continued, "If you're still with me, show up tomorrow at the new office. Bring your belief, bring your work ethic, and bring the mindset that says you were Made For More! That you're ready to write your next chapter."

I paused.

"And for those of you who need to walk away, I love you. I respect your decision. I understand this may not be your fight anymore. But for those of us ready to roll up our sleeves and find out what page turns next, my door is open. If more than twenty show up, we'll make it work."

The next morning, eighteen people showed up.

We didn't have a plan. The banks were still closing and people needed help. But we had grit. We had heart. And that was enough.

We fought hard. We grinded. We learned how to lead differently. And after six months, I realized something: I didn't want to go back to the old model. I didn't want to keep chasing the money. I wanted to chase Impact.

So I pivoted.

I launched a coaching program focused on training sales professionals. Not just to sell better, but to lead with heart. I built a framework called Sales Mind Map that I began teaching to mortgage professionals, insurance agencies, and real estate agents. Anyone who wanted to sell from a place of service.

That was the beginning of The NOW Academy in 2010. It was a company born not from strategy, but from surrender and soul. I wasn't building it to climb the corporate ladder again. I was building it to lift people up. What started as a coaching program quickly became one of the leading personal development platforms for speakers, authors, and coaches. It has since grown into a full-scale mentorship movement and also a publishing company called Impact Maker Publishing. There, we help changemakers bring their stories to life and launch movements that matter. I no longer chase someone else's dream. I wake up every day building the one God gave me!

I've failed forward more times than I can count. But that collapse, that storm—it was the one that taught me who I really was.

So if you're in the middle of a storm right now, if it feels like the roof is caving in and your whole world is slipping through your fingers, hear me when I say:

This is not the end of your story.

God does not waste pain. The plan isn't for you to quit. The plan isn't for you to drown. The plan is for you to come through the storm, wiser, stronger, and more grounded than ever.

This is not your final chapter. This is your plot twist. This is your breakthrough.

And friend, your time is *now*!

So let go of what you can't control. Take back the pen. And write what comes next.

"Faith without works is dead."
—James 2:17

You're not alone. Lean into prayer. Pray for your family. Pray for strength. Pray for peace. Pray for clarity. And if you run out of words, just sit quietly. God hears you.

We were never meant to carry this alone. Tap into your higher source. Trust that your cry doesn't fall on deaf ears. Prayer is not your last resort. It's your first weapon.

Let this chapter be your lifeline. I've walked through fire, and I promise you, there is light on the other side. If you're in a season of loss, addiction, collapse, or simply feeling unworthy, I want you to remember:

You are not what you've lost. You are what you rise into.

You were made for more. Your anchor is waiting. Hold fast. Let go of what you can't control. And choose to write your next chapter. One decision. One act of faith at a time.

Your time isn't later.

Your Time is NOW!

About the Author:

Brandon Hintz is a Husband, Father, Mentor, Speaker, Author, and breakthrough coach who helps leaders turn Their Message into Movements. As the founder of The NOW Academy, he empowers entrepreneurs and professionals to rise from adversity, lead with heart, and build purpose-driven businesses. Known for his real-talk coaching and unshakable faith, Brandon's mission is simple: to Help Others Realize they were Made for More...and Their Time is NOW!

Scan the QR Code to Learn More

My mission is to help new and existing online coaches build a bullet proof foundation so that they can transform their coaching business to make a bigger impact for those they help and reach 6 & 7 figures quickly.

Anchored in Vision and Infinite Faith

By Carey Conley

Now more than ever people are questioning why they're here. It's easy to drift and not know your real purpose in this life. Without purpose and a vision to fulfill it, you may find yourself adrift and anchorless. We live in a world now where you can pick up your device for five minutes and fall into comparison-mode, believing your peers are crushing it while you are falling behind. This is especially true with young adults.

When I was in my late twenties (in the mid to late '80s) most of us were told to get a good degree, find a good job, and work our way up the ranks. After graduating from college (good degree, check), my husband, Ross, and I were married. We then set our sights on the "good job." However, I found myself changing workplaces every two years because I didn't fit the 9-5 mold. Fortunately, I met a mentor who changed my life. She told me I could *create* the life I wanted; I just had to sit down and write out my own clear vision for my life. I immediately took out a legal pad and started writing.

I wrote about all the things I wanted for my life: a good relationship with my husband, a beautiful home, travel we would do together, the mom I wanted to be, and how I wanted to expand my own independence. I wanted residual, passive income and to work for a company with great leadership. I wanted to mentor and train other people. I also wanted to travel a lot! I got really clear on exactly what I wanted and the kind of person I wanted to become.

People often get worried when they can't see how their vision will play out or be fulfilled. I say write the vision, and the *how* will show up. After I wrote my first vision document, I continued working full time, had my son, Cole, and then became pregnant with my daughter, Laurel. I soon became a consultant for Arbonne, a network marketing company, because it checked all the boxes I had written in my vision.

When I started building my team at Arbonne, I invited all the leaders to meet with me and write their vision. I knew if they didn't have a powerful "why," they'd quit in a week. I continued to teach this vision practice to all my leaders over the next twenty years, and then I started facilitating workshops. I wrote my workbook, *Vision is Victory*, and people asked me to coach them. For the past fifteen years as an entrepreneurial coach, vision has been the foundation of my practice and my anchor in the storms of life.

My connection to God deeply rooted me in my faith and affirmed that the work I do is His calling for me. In all the years I was training and leading others in their visions, not knowing what was coming for me, I became very anchored in my purpose. The biggest storms I faced were losing my husband and son to suicide three years apart. It was a dark time, but when I look back, I can see each moment where I was supported and divinely connected. All the years of teaching and training, combined with God's love, formed an unshakeable foundation that kept me stable.

When people come to me and hear my story, they are often shocked. "How in the world did you get through that and still do what you do?"

I say, "I was already rooted in vision and purpose before all of this happened. The hard times actually accelerated what I've been doing as a speaker and entrepreneurial coach."

God's timing is amazing. Two nights before my husband passed, my business coach pulled me into a room of five other coaches and gave us the option to license her coaching program. I saw this as a beautiful opportunity because I didn't want to create a whole course for entrepreneurs. She had done it all for us. It was a beautiful example of two of my top values: collaboration and community.

I already had my vision built and knew the direction I was going to go. If I had not been so clear on wanting to teach vision to other people and having the vehicle to follow, I would have easily stopped working for a while when Ross passed. It was really healing for me to continue teaching and training at that point in my life.

Three years later, I lost my son to suicide. I had been living and working my vision for over twenty-five years, and I took a pause here to reevaluate where I was headed.

I have seen so many people walking around in the world doing what they were told to do and not what God's purpose is for them, and as a result, they feel very unsettled. Unfortunately most people will stay in a job just because they think that's what they're "supposed" to do, even though they are very unhappy and feel unimportant in the world. Sadly, I think a huge majority of us die that way.

Towards the end of my husband's life he was very successful and respected in corporate sales, and he had been with the same company for almost thirty years. But a couple things happened right before his passing. The kids had moved out and we were figuring out how to be empty nesters. At the same time his company was about to go through a merger, and he felt really scared about what that would mean for him. Truth be told, I think my husband was unhappy in corporate sales. Having witnessed the joy he experienced teaching Bible study to the kids at our church, I think he could have been a really great teacher. But because we were so ingrained in our lifestyle, he couldn't envision changing his work.

In a similar way, my son followed a path he thought he was supposed to, got a degree, and went to work for Channel 12, but I could see he was miserable inside. He would have thrived in a work environment where he could have been much more creative. However, like my husband, changing his job didn't feel like a "smart move," and making a change scared him to death. While I noticed each of their unhappiness when it came to their work, I want to be clear—suicide is a very complicated event; there's not just one cause.

Everyone reacts in different ways when they go through hard situations. Some people are good about going to group counseling, therapy, meeting up with friends, but after my husband and son passed on, I went inward. I kept up with the clients I had, but I stopped bringing in new ones. I really needed a lot of alone time, reflection, and quiet healing. It's important to know *you can deal with adversity however you need to.* If I didn't have my faith, my family, and my vision after they each passed, I would have been adrift in the storm.

Finding your community in the way that works for you is key when going through your own storms. I used to be much more outgoing and extraverted before my husband and son passed; now I am more selective about who I spend my time with. However, I do encourage people not to isolate themselves. You've got to find your people, whether through networking, specialized groups (I'm in several women's groups), church, or hobbies. Whatever—and whoever—brings you joy and helps you feel safe will help you heal.

I've also noticed the quality of people I spend my time with has changed. I've been more selective. I choose to be around people who feel safe, who are wiser than I am, who are purpose-driven, and who align with my mission. For example, there's a woman here in Arizona who has formed an organization called Helping Parents Heal. There were 1200 parents at the last event. All of the speakers are people who can bring messages forward from beyond. It's been an extremely powerful community to be part of.

I strongly recommend having people you trust to hold you accountable to your vision. I shared mine primarily with the women in Arbonne who were where I wanted to be. I knew they would encourage me on the days I wanted to quit. Two supportive women in my life who I call "my mamas" are Rita Davenport (past president of Arbonne and motivational speaker) and Sharon Lector (author, keynote speaker, and Business Master Mentor). Sharon also wrote the foreword for this book. These women have been instrumental in helping me be the leader I have become. You have to surround yourself with people who believe in you and your vision and remind you of it on the days that you can't see it.

Overall, the biggest lesson I have learned from my mentors, friends, clients, and experiences is to *write your vision from your heart*. What do you really want? What feels right in your soul? When I wrote out my whole vision, it was coming from deep within. If you don't know where to start, just start writing—it will reveal itself to you if you allow it.

I still coach entrepreneurs on vision today, especially those who don't have money or a gameplan. Now my passion project is serving young adults (early twenties to early thirties) who are struggling. Many young adults are really lost, and it's scary to see what's happening to many of them. My daughter is in this age range now, and my son was twenty-five when he passed. A lot of parents are seeking help for their young adult children. When I mention my passion for helping young adults in my vision talks, that's the topic that everyone comes to talk with me about in the back of the room afterwards. I am listening and creating a movement in this chapter of my life to help young adults feel loved, purposeful, and anchored in their truth.

Through my vision and faith, I know this life isn't all there is; as a Christian, I know I'll see my husband and son again. I believe life is infinite and endless. Infinity has always been my word, ever since I was young—from my company name, Infinity Corporation, to my Arbonne team. Infinite Nation. You may have noticed the infinity symbol combined with the anchor on the front of this book. To me, that image symbolizes being grounded in your faith for eternity. That, combined with a clear vision, is an anchor I know I can count on no matter what storm comes my way.

About The Author:

Carey Conley now travels the world and the country to virtual and live events helping men and women professionally and personally build their self-empowering skills by using her vision methodology. She shows them how to shed past pain, fear, and hardship, in order to manifest a beautiful life that's within reach. Carey Conley's personal story is full of extraordinary success and devastating tragedy. She lost her husband and son to suicide 3 years apart and was able to be strong for her daughter and to live her purpose that became her driving force. Those are the experiences that bring power to her message and help others achieve what they never thought was possible. Carey found her passion and ability to help men and women create, develop, and execute a rock-solid, bigger-than-life vision that propels them to succeed in all areas of life, including self-love, financial prosperity, a healthy lifestyle, caring relationships, a strong family, supreme confidence, and spiritual connection. She also co-authored a Bestselling book called 'Keep Looking Up' in 2019.

Scan the QR Code to Learn More:

In Vision is Victory, Carey Conley takes you on a journey to discover what has held you back from living your purpose and passion, and how to move beyond those walls to create a vision that is bigger than any obstacle you might encounter.

Speak Anyway

By Cathy Reilly

There are moments that change you—without warning, without permission, and often, without mercy.

For me, it wasn't just one moment. It was a slow unraveling. A thousand paper cuts of self-betrayal disguised as silence. The times I swallowed my words to keep the peace. The days I performed with strength while quietly questioning everything. The nights I replayed conversations in my head, wishing I had spoken up instead of shrinking down.

If you've ever felt that—like your voice was on the tip of your tongue but the world wasn't ready to hear it—then we already have something in common.

I built a life that looked solid on the outside, but I was crumbling inside. And I didn't even realize how much of myself I'd lost until I stood in the mirror one day and didn't recognize the woman staring back. I had followed all the "shoulds." I was successful by most standards. But I was living someone else's version of safe—saying yes when I meant no, saying nothing when I needed to speak, tolerating things I once said I never would.

Then I did something wild.

I sold my wedding ring and bought a horse.

Not because I needed an escape. I needed a mirror—something that would reflect the truth I'd been avoiding. That horse, BeauJo, wasn't a pet or a project. He became a partner in my healing. He showed me what real communication looked like. BeauJo didn't care about my titles or my trauma. He didn't care what I said. He responded to what I *meant*. He demanded presence. Honesty. Energy that matched the moment.

If I wasn't grounded, he wasn't following.
If I wasn't clear, he was confused.
If I wasn't connected, he simply didn't respond.

He didn't let me fake it. And honestly? I had been faking it for a long time.

That's the thing about adversity—it doesn't just test your circumstances. It tests your communication. It forces you to get honest about what you believe, what you tolerate, and what you're truly willing to say out loud.

And I wasn't saying much.

I had learned how to be agreeable, accommodating, and adaptable. I had built my identity around being the one who could handle it all. But I hadn't learned how to advocate for myself with clarity and courage. I hadn't learned how to set a boundary without apologizing for it. I hadn't learned how to say "I'm not okay" without feeling like a burden.

Until I did.

That realization cracked something open in me. I started speaking more honestly. First in private. Then in public. I started asking for what I needed. I stopped performing. I began practicing what I now call courageous clarity—the kind that doesn't require conflict but won't tolerate confusion either.

And what happened next was something I never expected—people started listening.

Not because I was polished. Not because I had all the answers. But because I was telling the truth. The real truth. The kind that makes people nod quietly because they've lived it too. The kind that reminds you—you're not alone.

Eventually, I started sharing my stories from the stage. And let me tell you—I was terrified. My knees shook. My voice cracked. My hands were clammy. But I did it anyway. I shared the moments I had hidden for so long: the betrayal, the heartbreak, the near-death experiences, the lessons learned from a horse who became my greatest teacher. I told the truth about what it looked like to lose your voice and fight to get it back.

And somewhere in the middle of the fear and the doubt, I found my power.

I turned those stories into lessons.
Those lessons became a keynote.
The keynote became a book.
The book became a training.
The training became a movement.

But none of that would've happened if I hadn't made one decision that terrified me:

To speak anyway.

Even when I didn't feel ready.
Even when I didn't know if it would land.
Even when I feared the judgment, the rejection, the fallout.

Because here's what I know now: Adversity doesn't define you. How you respond to it does.

And I choose to respond with voice. With clarity. With truth. Every time.

That doesn't mean I'm fearless. Please. I've cried in cars, overthought text messages, and had entire conversations with people in my head that I never had the nerve to speak out loud. But I've built a different relationship with fear. I don't let it silence me anymore. I let it sharpen me. Remind me what's at stake when I go quiet. Reconnect me with the reason I speak in the first place—to help others find their voice, too.

And sometimes, it's more than just empowerment. Sometimes, it's survival.

In 2016, I sneezed—and my world shifted.

Yes, you read that right. A sneeze. One sudden movement, and I felt pain like I'd never felt before. I couldn't breathe. I couldn't think straight. The old version of me might have waited it out. Might have dismissed it as stress or soreness or "I'll be fine." But something in me—the voice I'd spent years rebuilding—said, *No. Speak.*

So I did. I called my doctor. I called my family. I called my neighbor, who dropped everything and drove me to the emergency room. And thank God I did. The scans revealed blood clots covering both of my lungs. I was in serious danger. Timing was everything.

That day, my voice didn't just help me advocate for my needs. *It saved my life.*

And that's when I knew:

Your voice isn't just a tool.
It's a lifeline.
To your health.
To your power.
To your truth.

Today, I work with leaders, entrepreneurs, teams, and rising voices who want to speak with more impact, more confidence, more authenticity, and more trust. Not because they want to be loud—but because they want to be *clear*. And in a noisy, distracted, soundbite-driven world? Clarity is a superpower.

But here's the truth I tell every client, every audience, every person sitting quietly in the back of the room, wondering if their story matters:

You don't have to wait to be perfect to speak powerfully. You just have to stop waiting for permission.

Speak because your story deserves to be heard.
Speak because your boundaries deserve to be respected.
Speak because your truth is enough—even if your voice shakes when you say it.

This isn't about having the perfect words. It's about having the courage to use your words. To let go of the old scripts, the outdated stories, the armor you've been wearing to survive. And to let your voice rise—not as a performance, but as a *practice*.

And yes, it's a practice. You're going to mess it up. You're going to say the wrong thing. You're going to overshare, undershare, say too much, say it too late. But that's okay. You're not here to get it perfect.

You're here to get it *out*.

So if you're reading this and facing something hard right now . . . .
If you're sitting at the edge of a decision . . . .
If you're standing at a crossroads, wondering whether to stay quiet or say the hard thing . . . .

Let this be your sign.

Say it.
Say it scared.
Say it messy.
Say it with a lump in your throat.
Say it anyway.

Because the clarity you're craving won't come from thinking about it. It will come from choosing. From opening your mouth and speaking the truth that's been living inside you all along.

Speak for the version of you who once stayed silent.
Speak for the person watching you who's still afraid.
Speak for the future you who's already walking through the door you're scared to open.

I'm not here because I did it perfectly. I'm here because I did it anyway. And you can too.

Because what started as a whisper in me—a choice to speak, to stand, to stop shrinking—became something bigger. It became a calling. A message. A movement.

And it all started with a horse. My anchor.

BeauJo didn't just teach me to ride. He taught me to *lead*. He taught me to listen before I speak, to ground myself before I react, to stop hiding behind what's expected and start showing up in what's real.

When I was disconnected, he pulled away.
When I was calm, he leaned in.
When I was finally honest, he responded with trust.

That's what communication is—not a performance, but a relationship. Built moment by moment, with presence, energy, and truth.

The shift in me didn't come from reading more, doing more, or trying to be more. It came from *remembering who I already was*—and having the courage to speak from that place.

That's what BeauJo gave me. That's what I now give to others.

The movement I've built isn't about being louder. It's about being *clearer*.

It's about choosing voice over silence.
Truth over comfort.
Power over permission.

And it's about remembering that everything you want to become is already inside you—just waiting for you to speak it into existence.

About the Author:

Cathy Reilly is an international keynote speaker, podcast host, founder of The Clarity Code, and communication coach with 30+ years of experience in psychology, business, and law. She helps leaders and high-achieving professionals communicate with clarity, lead through change, and drive lasting results. Known for her direct, relatable style, Cathy equips individuals and teams to navigate high-stakes conversations, strengthen presence, and create meaningful, sustainable growth—personally and professionally.

Scan the QR Code to Learn More:

If you're ready to elevate your communication, strengthen your presence, and lead with clarity, you are invited to download my communication frameworks or I'd be honored to gift you my time—visit here for more.

The Life I Didn't Plan

By Dani M. Peterson

There are seasons in life when nothing makes sense—when everything familiar becomes unrecognizable. I found myself in one of those seasons after the truth surfaced in my first marriage. It didn't come all at once, but slowly, over nearly two decades—through deception, hidden compulsions, and the painful fallout of sexual addiction.

I was in shock and could barely breathe. It felt like I was in free fall, with no ground beneath me. My mind was spinning—my mental and emotional well-being in turmoil. I was screaming inside, asking, "*What just happened? How is this my life?*"

The life I had built, believed in, and fought for unraveled before my eyes. From the outside, things looked "fine." I was a stay-at-home mom, raising two children, doing all the right things. But inside our home—and inside my heart—cracks had long been forming. When everything finally came to light, it wasn't a sudden collapse. It was more like a slow erosion—a thousand tiny heartbreaks I hadn't known how to name until the truth was undeniable.

My mind felt hijacked—spinning with more questions and on constant high alert. I moved through the motions, showing up for my kids, smiling when needed. But inside, I was unraveling. A weight pressed on my chest constantly. Panic, grief, confusion, and rage pulsed through me—sometimes all at once, sometimes in unpredictable waves. I questioned everything—my marriage, my worth, my ability to trust. I even questioned God. What was He up to? My faith, once steady and comforting, now felt tangled in the wreckage. And yet, something in me held on. Not perfectly. Not with clarity. But with a deep, aching desire to believe that God would get me and my kids through this—to find some kind of meaning, even in the darkness.

And underneath it all, one question echoed louder than the rest: *Why?* I longed to wake up and find it had all been a bad dream. But it wasn't. There were no simple answers. The only way forward was through.

What's kept in darkness doesn't stay contained. Deception and hidden compulsions don't just affect the one holding the secrets—they spread like cracks beneath the surface of a relationship. Sexual addiction distorts trust, warps intimacy, and creates an invisible but undeniable distance. For the one who discovers it, there's a rupture in reality: confusion, shame, and the sense that your entire history is now up for question. The fallout isn't limited to the betrayer's struggle—it devastates the emotional safety, connection, and integrity of the relationship itself. Facing this truth was part of my healing. It didn't erase the pain, but it helped me name what I was up against—and that naming became the beginning of reclaiming my voice and my future.

The shift didn't come as a lightning bolt or dramatic revelation. It came quietly. A single breath. A whispered prayer. A moment of stillness. An inner knowing, below what my mind could comprehend.

For a long time, I resisted the pain—tried to outrun it, reason with it, spiritualize it, even suppress it. But pain has a way of surfacing, no matter how deeply we try to bury it. Eventually, I understood I had a choice: continue surviving . . . or begin the slow, deliberate work of healing. At first, that meant simply telling the truth—to myself. About what had happened. About what I had tolerated. About the ache I carried that no one else could see.

I didn't have a map. But I had a longing—to come home to myself and to experience God differently, not through performance or pretending, but through presence. That meant stepping outside familiar spaces and trying things I once dismissed. I found my way to yoga, breathwork, and meditation. These weren't part of the faith vocabulary I'd grown up with—but they became necessary. They helped quiet the chaos, reconnect me to my body, and create space for grief and grace to coexist.

The more I slowed down, the more I could feel again—not just the pain, but small, steady flickers of life within me. Healing wasn't about controlling the outcome. It was about witnessing. Being present. Honoring what hurt without rushing to fix it. This was not easy for me.

There were moments of clarity—glimpses of who I was beyond the pain. Moments when I remembered I didn't have to earn my worth. That I could use my voice. That I could breathe again—not just through my lungs, but through my life. It wasn't one turning point. It was many—strung together by intention, grace, and a growing conviction that my story wasn't over.

Healing didn't arrive all at once or wrapped in certainty. It came in pieces—fragile, messy, and sacred. Over time, the fog lifted just enough for me to start rebuilding—not the life I had before, but the life I was meant to live. I did it while parenting two children. Alone. I homeschooled, worked multiple jobs, and did my best to keep their world steady while mine continued to shake. I showed up every day with love and presence, knowing there would be gaps.

There were nights I cried after they were asleep, wondering how I'd get through the next day. But somehow, I did. I surrendered. I trusted—sometimes by the hour—that God would meet me where I lacked and that He would meet my kids where they needed Him most. And He did. Over and over again.

Even when I wasn't sure what I believed anymore about life, love and marriage, I felt God with me—not in grand gestures but in quiet currents beneath the chaos. A song on the radio. An unexpected check when bills were due. A stranger's kindness. A truth that settled in my spirit when I wasn't looking for it. These were love notes from the Divine—reminders I wasn't alone. God didn't pull me out of the fire. He stood with me in it. And that presence—even in my fear and doubt—was my anchor.

Scriptures I had long known began to take on new meaning:

"For I know the plans I have for you," declares the Lord, "plans to prosper you and not to harm you, plans to give you a future and a hope."
—Jeremiah 29:11

"Trust in the Lord with all your heart and lean not on your own understanding; in all your ways acknowledge Him, and He shall direct your paths."
—Proverbs 3:5–6

"The Lord Himself goes before you and will be with you; He will never leave you nor forsake you."
—Deuteronomy 31:8

These words didn't erase the pain—but they steadied me. Prayer and Scripture kept my heart open. And the practices I once resisted became sacred entry points—pathways back to myself. Yoga helped calm the panic. Breathwork helped me release it. Meditation helped me hear what lived beneath the noise.

I let go of the lie that my worth depended on someone else's choices. I gave myself space to grieve, to rest. And slowly, I began to rebuild—not into the person I had been, but into someone new. Grounded. Awake. Still healing—but whole.

God was never absent from my pain. He was there—in the silence, in the questions, in the moments I wrestled, and when it felt like I had nothing left in me to keep me going. He sent signs, people, provisions—exactly when I needed them, even if I couldn't see it right away.

"The wound is the place where the Light enters you."
—Rumi

I'm living proof that light can find its way in—even through the deepest cracks.

If your world feels shattered—if you're just trying to make it through the day—I want you to know: there is life on the other side. It may not look like the life you planned. But it can be a life rooted in truth, resilience, and a deeper connection to God, yourself and others than you ever thought possible. You don't have to rush your healing. You don't need to have it all figured out. You can feel like you are falling apart and still be worthy of peace, love, and rest. Healing isn't about fixing what's broken. It's about meeting yourself—honestly and gently—again and again. Choosing courage over comfort. Presence over perfection. Faith over fear.

Trauma doesn't get the final word. Betrayal isn't the end of your story. Rebuilding is possible, even when everything has been reduced to rubble. Healing isn't linear—it circles, spirals, surprises. But each turn builds strength, resilience, and the capacity to be with what unfolds. Pain, I've learned, can become the soil where purpose takes root.

You are not too far out of God's reach. He has more for you. Lean in. Believe. He's got you.

No question—my life didn't turn out the way I once expected. But it's a life I've lived fully, wrestled with deeply, and grown into. Every experience, even the ones that nearly broke me, has shaped who I am today. I've learned to feel pain without letting it define me, and to release what once held me captive. I've made peace with the past—not by pretending it didn't happen, but by learning to see it through a different lens. I've come home to parts of myself I thought were lost—and I live from that place now: more honest, more whole.

Anchored in Truth and sustained by daily practices, I continue to grow, staying present and aligned with the woman I was always meant to be. And what once felt like the end of my story has become the beginning of a new calling. What were some of my darkest moments now fuel my mission to come alongside other women and couples traveling this difficult road—not because I have all the answers, but because I know what it means to find solid ground again and why I keep showing up—with compassion, hope, and truth.

About the Author:

Dani Peterson is an accredited and certified specialist and holistic practitioner. She supports individuals navigating some of life's darkest and painful moments — like infidelity, sex addiction, and problematic compulsive behaviors. Dani guides women through heartbreak and couples, as they find their way back to one another or gently apart, when the road calls them in different directions.

She's a wife, mom, and nonna who loves all things Italian and Enzo her Wire Fox Terrier.

Scan the QR Code to Learn More:

If your world has been turned upside down by betrayal and you're not sure where to begin, Betrayed 101** is a free mini-series** designed to help you take your first steps. It offers clarity, honest guidance and the hope that healing and restoration are possible. Need further guidance? Schedule a free 30-min Consultation call today!

The Storm of Self-Abandonment: Reclaiming Who You Are

By Jillian Verdun

Have you ever reached a point in life where you quietly whisper to yourself, "I don't even know who I am anymore"? If so, you are not alone. Many of us experience the silent storm of self-abandonment. It doesn't roar loudly, but instead creeps in quietly, slowly draining us of our identity. We become masters of adapting, adjusting, and accommodating to fit the expectations and desires of others, while unknowingly losing the very essence of who we are.

For much of my life, I lived in this storm.

From the outside, I had it all together. I had just closed on a beautiful new home in 2007. I had a good job, a steady income, and I kept a smile on my face for everyone who needed it. That smile became part of my armor: polished, presentable, and never slipping.

But behind closed doors, the cracks were beginning to show. Just days after moving in, my car was vandalized at work during my lunch break, a personal violation that left me shaken. My brand-new washing machine flooded the foyer of my new home. Then in 2012, everything I had worked so hard for financially, materially, and relationally, nearly collapsed. Life kept throwing curveballs, and while each one seemed manageable on its own, the weight of them all began to quietly crush me.

I was the dependable one, the fixer, the peacekeeper, always available for others, but rarely available for myself. I had been living in a kind of emotional lockdown for years, keeping my guard up, hiding my struggles, and pushing down fear, shame, resentfulness, and anger as if they didn't exist. I had grown so good at adapting to what everyone else needed that I stopped asking what I needed. My dreams didn't matter. My voice got quieter. Eventually, I forgot what it even sounded like.

This is how self-abandonment begins: with small compromises. I said "yes" when I meant "no," silenced my opinions to avoid conflict, and suppressed my dreams to maintain peace. Over time, these choices became patterns, and these patterns became habits. I changed into versions of myself that others found comfortable, abandoning my God-given uniqueness in the process.

I believed the only way to be successful and find peace was to work harder—not smarter, just harder. I told myself I couldn't say yes to anything I might fail at because failure would mean I wasn't good enough. I equated worth with performance. And when you live like that, even love starts to feel like a job description.

We adopt different roles to survive:

- The Chameleon: shifting personality and beliefs to blend in.
- The Caretaker: constantly prioritizing others' needs over our own.
- The Achiever: overperforming to prove our worth.
- The Peacemaker: avoiding conflict at the expense of truth.

I had played all those roles. But they didn't fill the emptiness. They only helped me function. Not succeed. Just function.

Therapy didn't stick for long. Books helped for a moment, but didn't reach the places I was too scared to name. Self-reflection exercises helped when I was completely honest with myself. I didn't have many people I could confide in, and the few I did trust, I didn't want to burden. So, I cried in silence and showed up in public with a flawless smile. That's what I thought strength looked like.

And then I broke.

After a deep and painful breakup, I realized something: I had lost myself. Again. I had invested in that relationship for all the wrong reasons, not because it felt right to me, but because I was listening to what other people thought I should do. I ignored my first mind, the intuition that tried to protect me. I adapted, adjusted, and performed for approval. And I didn't just do that in romance. I noticed that same pattern showing up in all my relationships throughout my life.

I had given so much of myself away, molding, bending, becoming whatever others needed, that I couldn't even recognize who I was anymore. I wasn't dreaming. I wasn't living. I was just moving through the motions, trying not to fall apart.

That was my breaking point.

At the core of this struggle lies fear. Fear of rejection. Fear of being unloved. Fear of conflict. Fear of not being enough. I believed that if I could just keep everyone happy, I'll finally feel secure and accepted. But in trying to win love and approval, I sacrificed my authentic self. And the love I received, though real, never fully satisfied because it wasn't aimed at the real me. It was aimed at the version I created.

There's a quiet devastation that comes with realizing you've become a stranger to yourself. And it doesn't fix itself overnight. My healing didn't happen quickly. In fact, it took more than a decade, from 2007 until 2018, to fully reclaim my identity.

That day, in 2018, something inside me shifted. It wasn't loud. It wasn't dramatic. But I finally felt like myself again. I said "no" in a complete sentence, without explanation, and I meant it. I stopped apologizing for needing rest, space, or truth. I stopped hiding the parts of me I once believed would be judged or rejected. I stopped carrying shame for how long it took me to come back home to myself.

That's the real turning point: when I stopped hiding and started honoring the real me. I had to unlearn the belief that my worth was tied to how much I did for others. I had to face the discomfort of disappointing people. But on the other side of that discomfort was a peace and confidence I had never known. I began to live from a place of purpose, not performance. I no longer needed to earn love because I finally understood that I was already deeply loved for who I am, not for what I do.

Sometimes reclaiming yourself will feel lonely. I found that certain relationships didn't survive my growth. But I remembered this: anything built on my false self was never meant to last. What is rebuilt on the other side of my courage is stronger, richer, and more grounded in truth.

I realized how many people I had unintentionally pushed away during that season of silence and survival. Not because I didn't love them, but because I was so focused on performing strength that I didn't leave room for vulnerability. That awareness humbled me and made me more intentional with the way I show up now, softer, clearer, and more grounded.

Today, I stand proud of the woman I've become. Not because I'm perfect, but because I've done internal work to become whole again. I know what it's like to lose yourself in love, in survival, in performance. And I know what it takes to come back.

Now, when I smile, it's real. When I say "yes," it's rooted. When I say "no," it's enough.

You may face resistance as you reclaim yourself. Some people have benefited from your self-abandonment and may not welcome your growth. But protecting your peace is not selfish, it is sacred. You cannot fully serve others when you are spiritually and emotionally depleted. Boundaries are not walls to keep people out. They are gates that protect what is valuable within.

Here is the truth: you don't need permission to be who you are. God already gave it to you. Philippians 4:13 reminds us, "I can do all things through Christ who strengthens me." The strength you need is already in you. You just have to trust it.

Reclaiming who you are is not just about doing less for others. It's about doing more of what aligns with who God created you to be. It's about showing up in your truth, even if your voice trembles. It's about saying, "I matter," not in arrogance, but in wholehearted alignment with your worth.

There is life after losing yourself—a full, free, authentic life. You can love again. You can trust again. You can dream again. And more than anything, you can choose you again.

That's the real success story.

The work I do today helping women reclaim control over their money and their power, is a direct reflection of this journey. Because once you find your voice again, you can't help but help others find theirs too.

About the Author:

Jillian Verdun, founder of JMV Financial Services, has been helping clients navigate financial challenges since 2007 with integrity, personal care, and proven strategies. Passionate about making finances simple, she empowers entrepreneurs to manage their money and grow their businesses with confidence. Jillian holds a Bachelor's degrees in Accounting and Computer Information Systems, a Master's in Accounting, and is a Sacred Money Archetype Coach, speaker, and author. She serves as the calm in any financial storm.

Scan the QR Code to Learn More:

Discover your Sacred Money Archetype and uncover how your natural habits influence how you spend, save, and earn. Gain clarity to build financial freedom in alignment with your true self.

Generation Why & the Power of Making an Impact

By Jordan Miller

I am Jordan Miller—artist, husband, father, and Executive Director of the best, most impactful and life-changing nonprofit around—Generation Why or GNWY (Gen – Y). You may be asking, how can this guy proclaim to lead the best nonprofit around? Well, it is because the birth of this organization literally helped save my life, and the concept of Generation Why Co. arose from a need that hit very close to home. This is where my story begins.

I'm the only child of the most loving, most hard-working parents in the world, and I was a happy kid. As I grew up, my mother taught me how to love people and my dad taught me a good work ethic. In school I took drama class, played the drums, and participated in sports. I was raised in the church, and no matter what, my faith in God is my foundation. I love to draw and write stories, and when I worked at a local sandwich shop, I would write stories and raps and spoken words on the receipts.

While I had a great childhood, several of my friends did not. They were dealing with physical abuse, emotional abuse, and drugs, and they always came to me with their problems. Because they were my chosen family, I tended to take on their problems without realizing that that weight was not mine to carry, and it shaped a lot of my writing. After graduating from high school, all of those friends left and went to major colleges while I was working a forty-hour per week job, taking community college classes, and doing an internship as well. Those friends never knew that I still carried their problems with me.

The whole time I was still trying to figure out what I wanted to do with my life. I was introduced to the culture of hip-hop, and I began traveling with music and a DJ just trying to share my story. This is the time when my story took a turn and the storm began.

All I knew that I was good at was loving people well (which I learned from my mom), but community college did not have that as a degree. While I was traveling and performing, I realized that I was already doing what I wanted to do. Unfortunately, my parents did not fully understand. To them, that didn't sound like a plan for my life. In addition to my parents' lack of support and the emotional baggage I was still carrying for my friends, I was battling my own demons and thoughts. For example, my inner demons said things like, "If you're not good enough, what you're doing is not going to impact anybody. This dream of yours is not going to be sustainable for your future."

And that is where I entered the lowest part of my life. I had never battled with depression or anxiety or thoughts of suicide, but all of those thoughts and feelings came to me all at once. Wow, this was a new thing for me. Not a whole lot of people from my hometown dealt with these things. It was never talked about in the church. So I kept stuffing all of these feelings down until one night it became too much. During my freshman year of college, I attempted suicide twice. Obviously I am writing this and a survivor of suicide. Thank you, God!

But it didn't stop there. A year or two later I lost one of my friends that I graduated with to suicide. Speaking about this story still affects me to this day. I speak about this story in the schools, because this was also a turning point for me. Have you ever lost somebody that you cared about— someone who you thought had everything together and would be the next president? This is how that loss felt for me.

I truly believe there is a life degree for loving people—getting your masters in empathy. My parents love and serve their friends, no matter what they've done, working late nights for other people, and doing whatever it takes to help others. They are where I learned my masters in empathy.

The reason the loss of this friend affected me so much was that my friend messaged me on Facebook a couple months before his passing, and I never messaged him back. I would give anything to take thirty seconds out of my day to message him, check in on him, and just see his face one more time.

A year after his passing a statistic hit in our home state of Oklahoma. Our state went from thirty-second to the third leading state in the nation for suicide. Now having already dealt with this personally, overcoming those thoughts, emotions, and actions, the thoughts of my friend's passing the previous year struck a chord with me that cannot be explained, but with it came an urgency and a calling from God.

Some people think a calling can be a burden, but I believe everything in life is about perspective. You can take the good times and the bad times of life and be grateful for them and take them as wins and lessons, instead of taking them as wins and losses—all from simply changing your perspective. For me, my calling became my anchor.

This was the next turning point for me. Taking all of my experience of traveling and performing with my close friends, putting on shows and spreading light to crowds all over the nation, I wanted to change the approach and do something to help Oklahoma and the many students there who are searching—for life, for a purpose, for a *why*.

This is when I felt the name Generation Why in my heart. We wanted to do more than wake up a generation. We wanted to provide life for them, a reason to get up, a reason to live. So in 2017, we made it official.

With a group of young college kids, we hit the road, traveling around Oklahoma in our personal cars with multiple people and rental sound equipment. We started to see these students whenever we came into their school—changing the environment, and coming in with a full production of lights, sound equipment, screens, a DJ, professional dancers, rappers, spoken word artists, and motivational speakers. Now being from Oklahoma, this is something that normally does not come from our state with idols such as Reba McEntire, Toby Keith, and Blake Shelton. We definitely came into the schools with a different approach: meeting them where they're at, speaking on their level. Inspiring them with our strengths and connecting through our weaknesses, we have story after story of students being impacted by the experience of Generation Why.

So much so, we have even had students come up to us, crying, telling us how much the message meant to them, and handing over suicide letters that they wrote in the class period before that. After a presentation in Michigan, a girl came up and said, "Because you were here today, now I can be here tomorrow," and handed over her suicide note that she had in her bag. If that doesn't light a fire in you, I don't know what will.

This group of young college kids, including myself, have been figuring it out along the way. I didn't go to school for nonprofit work. I didn't know how to lead teams or create systems or grow an organization. All I knew was how to love people.

And that love has grown a team of fifteen people over the past six years. Our organization has traveled all over the nation impacting over 150,000 students in person, and now millions online as well. Our organization and mission have evolved, and we have built another branch onto the organization with a year-round class in a school here in the city, teaching, mentoring, and doing life with the students. We are looking to grow and put this class in schools all over America.

We also have built a social media platform, organically, impacting millions online—creating skits, motivational tips, funny concepts, dance videos, and inspiring content that the students are able to wake up to every morning and follow throughout their day. Social media can be a tool for great impact and change if you use it correctly and don't consume it constantly. As creators we can create an escape for our audience, or we can create an enclosure for them.

Generation Why provides an escape, a safe place, something to look forward to, an experience that is life-changing for students.

You never know how much impact you will make until you remove yourself from the day-to-day grind, remove yourself from yourself, and look at all that you and your team have accomplished. That's the biggest thing: you cannot do it alone. I would not be here if it was not for this amazingly dedicated and crazy-ambitious team.

We all see the vision because we see the need. Where is the need in your life? Where is the need in your world? You may not have a solution, but you sure as hell have a voice and a gift that you can use to help heal that need. At GNWY it is our duty and responsibility to be all things for all people, as well as impact all people through all the things.

This chapter is also a mental health check up. If you are in a low spot, promise me you'll talk to somebody. Surround yourself with people that not only gas you up, but will hold you up and hold you accountable to the things that you say and that you want to accomplish.

We are all on a journey, and I am glad that our paths have crossed. I would love to connect with you and invite you along on our journey. We are on the path to purpose—pursuing life, spreading joy, and changing students' lives. So I hope and pray that you pursue your Why as we pave out. Peace.

About the Author:

Jordan Miller is the CEO and Founder of *Generation Why*, a nonprofit focused on youth mental health and wellbeing. A multi-talented creative and educator, Jordan is a Hip-Hop and spoken word artist, motivational speaker, DJ, author, and father. After surviving two suicide attempts and losing a close friend to suicide, Jordan launched Generation Why to create a space for healing, connection, and empowerment. With over 16 years in the arts and 11 years mentoring youth across the nation, he and his team have impacted over 150,000 lives. Featured in Forbes and on local news outlets like News 9 and Fox 25, Jordan is also an accredited speaker through the American Foundation for Suicide Prevention and a published writer in *Social Spark*. His mission: to inspire and uplift every generation through creativity, purpose, and education.

Scan the QR Code to Learn More:

Students lives matter as well as their voices. With over a decade of experience within the school system, Generation Why has curated a life giving program provoking the minds and hearts of the future. Come be a part of breaking the stigma around mental health.

Anchored in Adversity—The Moment That Made the Mission

By Dr. Julie Ducharme

I sat in the quiet hospital room, listening to the steady beep of my mother's heart monitor—each sound growing fainter. She had been there for twelve days. What began as an infection had spiraled out of control, leading to a stroke and heart attack. I had been praying for God to heal her, to perform a miracle. But somewhere along the way, my prayer shifted. I began asking God to take her home, to relieve her of the suffering that had overtaken her body. The doctors had told us she would never recover—she would live the rest of her life in a vegetative state.

I leaned in close and whispered, "Mom, it's okay to go. I promise I'll take care of Dad, of Shelly, of Paul, and all the grandkids." It felt like I was begging her to let go, to stop fighting, to find peace. Deep down, I still wanted a miracle. I still didn't want to say goodbye. But I knew—I knew she had to go.

Our family gathered around her. I held her hand as her breathing slowed. At first, her face looked afraid. Then she took one final breath . . . and she was gone. A wave of peace washed over her face, and in that moment, something inside me broke. I'll never forget that moment for as long as I live.

Your life changes forever when you witness someone's soul leave their body. I knew I would never be the same. Holding the person you love most as they take their last breath—it's nothing short of earth-shattering.

At my mother's memorial service, we expected her church friends to come. What I didn't expect were the others—the people no one else had time for, the ones I had once said were taking advantage of her. And yet, they came. Not just to pay respects, but to weep. The room overflowed with people she had quietly helped—people she had loved when no one else would.

At that moment, a question hit me hard: *Who would show up at my funeral? Who would weep for me? What kind of legacy was I leaving behind?* I didn't have an answer—and that realization shook me.

I saw, maybe for the first time, that I hadn't been living a life of impact. I had judged the very people my mother embraced. I thought they didn't deserve her kindness. But I was wrong. So wrong.

My mother wasn't famous. She didn't hold a title in a big organization or speak on stages. But she was a giant in my life. She led without ever needing the spotlight. She taught me that leadership wasn't about control—it was about service.

I watched her care for our family, our neighbors, people in need, people who didn't have anyone else. I watched her give without waiting for applause. She was love in motion, grace with grit. And to this day, she is the single greatest example of servant leadership I've ever known.

Her legacy wasn't built in a corporate office or on social media. It was built in kitchens, church pews, hospital rooms, school hallways—in all the places people just needed someone to see them, help them, and believe in them.

She showed me that power doesn't always look like what the world celebrates. Sometimes, power is quiet. It listens more than it speaks. It lifts rather than dominates. It heals.

When I lost my mother, it shattered me.

It was more than grief. It was as though the person who kept me tethered to my center—who helped me believe I could always find my way back no matter how far I wandered—was gone. For months, I moved through life like a ghost. I ran my companies. I taught my classes. I smiled at events. But inside, I was breaking.

She had always been my moral compass, my sounding board; my reminder that kindness and strength could co-exist. Without her, I wasn't just heartbroken—I was *unmoored*. And yet . . . her voice didn't leave me. Her legacy didn't either. Even in the deepest valley of grief, I began to feel something stir. It was faint at first, like the memory of a song—but it grew louder each day. She hadn't raised me to collapse in loss. She had raised me to *lead through it*.

Up until that point, my mission had been successful. I wanted to build businesses, reach goals, earn credibility in spaces that often shut women out. But in the wake of her passing, everything shifted. My purpose was no longer just about what I could accomplish—it became about *who I could serve*.

I no longer cared about approval; I cared about impact. I wanted to build something that would make her proud. Something that wouldn't just echo her legacy—but multiply it. I went deeper into my faith. I asked God not just to heal me, but to *use* me. I began saying yes to things that scared me, and no to things that once validated me.

The journey ahead of me over the next twelve years was anything but easy. I thought I understood what it meant to be a servant leader—but I quickly realized this transformation would be like walking through fire. Every time I hit a wall, I instinctively reached for the phone to call my mom . . . only to remember I couldn't. That ache never really faded.

I had to learn how to redefine myself without her voice guiding me and remember the lessons she taught me and the conversations we had. I longed for a woman mentor, a mother figure—someone to step in, offer wisdom, and tell me I was going to be okay.

It was just me and God on that road. And through each struggle, each prayer, each quiet moment, I began to discover who I was really meant to be—the woman I wanted to become. I often asked myself: *Am I even worthy to carry the legacy she left behind?* That question didn't go away . . . but slowly, I began to live the answer.

And slowly, a new vision emerged.

Not just for a business.
Not just for a platform.
But for a *global movement.*

The idea started as a whisper as if my mother was whispering in my ear: *What if you created a space for women like I did, but this time give them the platform to speak.* But as women often do, I fought the idea that I was the one to do this. Besides my mother's death, nothing major or traumatic had ever happened in my life, at least compared to other women's stories. I didn't feel like I had a story to share. Imposter syndrome reared its ugly head, and I kept saying no until I couldn't. Until something happened at my job that made me realize I had spent years watching talented women be passed over, talked over, or told they were too much or not enough. I had been one of them.

I had to speak up for women like me who were fighting to have a space, a voice. I knew the way women treated each other had to change. I took a note out of my mother's playbook—kindness, love, and connection—and thought, could we create something like this for everyone like me who does have a story, who does feel minimized, and who does not know how to rise up to embrace their true authentic self?

My mother had a gift; she could see women's worth and knew how to pull it out of them. That whisper had become a loud voice yelling in my ear. So I created Lead and Empower Her SHE Talks. It wasn't just an event. It was a platform. A microphone. We launched with one goal: to give women everywhere the opportunity to rise—by speaking, by leading, by writing, by owning their story. It took off. It's hard to believe it is eight years old now. It's hard to believe that we are not just operating in the United States but all over the world..

We women are the same, we have the same dreams, aspirations, struggles, and share many of the same issues. I know my mother is smiling up above because she knew I could connect women worldwide. Sadly, I had to lose my mom to change the world for women. Although I miss her, I understand now why God sometimes lets us lose good people in our lives. In order for us to grow we have to lose them, or even let our old self die to see our new self grow and thrive.

SHE Talks is successful not because of me—but because women were *ready*. They didn't need to be told what to do. They needed to be reminded who they already were.

Today I run six companies, and SHE Talks is one of them. If you had asked me if I would have been here twelve years ago I would have said, no way! The vision I had was so much smaller than what God had planned for me. People often ask me how I do it all—multiple businesses, speaking, teaching, and leading a global movement.

The answer is: I don't do it *alone.*

I am anchored by three things:

1. **Faith:** My relationship with God is what carries me through every high and every valley. My faith reminded me during my mother's passing that death isn't the end of the story. It's the beginning of legacy. It reminded me that I'm not here by accident, and neither is this calling.
2. **Family:** My father taught me discipline, sacrifice, and perseverance. My husband, Josh, is the steady wind behind everything I do. He believes in my mission—and reminds me of it when I forget. Together, we've built not just businesses, but a way of life that allows our family to thrive in joy, service, and freedom.
3. **Fueling Others:** What fills me now is not accolades—it's activation. Watching a woman stand on stage for the first time and declare her truth . . . seeing a student finally believe they can succeed . . . helping an entrepreneur take the leap into ownership. Those are my fuel. Every time I give someone else the mic, I'm reminded that *this is exactly where I'm meant to be.*

When I look back over the last twelve years since my mom passed I realize:

Adversity could have broken me.

Grief could've ended me.

You don't need to wait until you have it all figured out. The truth is, your platform may already be inside your pain. I never planned to start a global movement. I just followed the thread of my mother's legacy. I listened to the whisper of God's prompting. And I trusted that what hurt most could also heal others. That's the path of a servant leader. It's not always loud. It's not always visible. But it *is* always powerful. When you dare to rise, you don't just shift your own life—you shift what's possible for everyone watching.

About the Author:

Dr. Julie Ducharme is a national best-selling author, speaker, professor, and entrepreneur with 20+ years of experience. She leads the SHE Talks movement, empowering women to speak and lead boldly. As founder of JD Consulting, she helps businesses grow through creative marketing. A champion for education and leadership, Dr. Ducharme inspires others through her work, teaching, and publications to rise, lead, and make a meaningful impact.

Scan the QR Code to Learn More:

If something inside you is stirring—an ache, a calling, a quiet whisper—don't ignore it. Now is the time to rise, speak, and lead from the very place that once broke you—because your mission is waiting.

The Power of Hope Through Community

By Karen and Chris Laos

Chris:

"Your kidneys are failing rapidly," the doctor said, his voice measured but grave. "We need to start dialysis within a few months."

The words hit me like a physical blow. I was still recovering from a stroke, thinking I was coming out of the storm, not heading into a deeper one. My body had already betrayed me once. Now it was happening again—only this time, the path ahead felt darker and more uncertain than anything I had ever faced.

I didn't know then how much I would need the people around me. I didn't realize that hope doesn't survive in isolation—it grows in community.

Karen:

I remember exactly where I was when he told me. Parked along the road in San Diego, sitting in my rental car, about to walk into a speaking engagement.

"The doctor says my kidneys are failing and I need to go on dialysis."

My jaw dropped in disbelief. We had just started seeing light again after his stroke. Now this? That historic day in February 2020 will forever be etched in my memory. Our lives were changing in real time, and I had no blueprint for what lay ahead.

What would this mean for my new speaking business? I had just left my corporate job, and now our world was being upended. The questions multiplied faster than I could process them.

Chris:

The transition to peritoneal dialysis felt overwhelming from the start. We chose PD because I could do it at home—more flexibility. But what I didn't realize was how completely it would take over every corner of our lives.

The boxes started arriving like clockwork. IV fluids stacked from floor to ceiling in our bedroom. A machine appeared beside our bed that would become my nightly tether. I warned Karen: "You're not going to like this."

Those first few months were brutal. Dialysis became my new reality—connecting to the machine every night, following a strict schedule that governed our entire household. Simple pleasures like eating became complex calculations of phosphorus and potassium levels. But the physical challenges paled in comparison to the psychological warfare I waged with despair.

Karen:

He wasn't kidding about me not liking it.

I hate clutter. I love calm, organized spaces. But suddenly, our home looked like a medical storage unit. The visual reminder of his illness was everywhere. I didn't have time to ease into caregiving. One moment I was organizing keynote presentations, and the next I was learning life-saving procedures.

Those stacks of medical supplies felt like they were closing in on me. This disease had invaded our world, changing how we spent our evenings, how we traveled, how we thought about the future. We did our best to laugh, to pray, to keep living. But I had quiet moments where I felt like I couldn't catch my breath, struggling under the burden of watching my husband suffer while feeling powerless to fix it.

Chris:

The darkest part wasn't the physical pain—it was the nights when hope felt foreign. There were evenings when I lay awake, tethered to that machine, wondering if it would ever get better. The thoughts that crept in weren't dramatic declarations but quiet whispers: What if I just stopped treatment? What if I simply let go?

These weren't abstract questions. They were real temptations that settled into my mind like unwelcome guests. Despair wasn't an emotion—it was a presence that could fill a room and make breathing feel like a conscious choice.

During these moments, I understood hopelessness as something tangible—something that whispered lies about my worth, my future, my ability to endure. But even in the deepest valleys, I was never truly alone. Three anchors held me steady: my faith in Jesus, my incredible wife Karen, and a community that refused to let this illness define or destroy me.

Karen:

I saw it all—the weariness in his eyes, the weight he carried. And I carried my own invisible load. Chris had always been the rock in our relationship, but now I had to become his anchor. When I couldn't carry the full weight alone, our church family stepped in.

They didn't just offer prayers—they offered presence. Meals when I was too exhausted to cook. Rides when I couldn't be in two places at once. Encouragement when my own faith wavered. And hugs—so many hugs, because that's Chris's love language.

That's what I've learned about hope. It's not always loud or triumphant. Sometimes, it's just showing up. Holding on. Sitting in the dark with someone until the light returns.

Chris:

One moment stands out like a beacon: April 6, 2020. I had just undergone surgery to have my dialysis catheter implanted—a procedure that made the reality undeniably permanent. Karen was driving me home, and I sat quietly, feeling defeated and emotionally drained.

But as we turned the corner onto our street, I saw something that stopped my breath: dozens of people lining our sidewalk, holding homemade signs, clapping, cheering. My church family, neighbors, friends—they had gathered for a declaration.

They were announcing to me, to the neighborhood, to the universe itself, that this disease would not define me, would not defeat me, would not have the final word in my story. In that moment, I understood something profound: hope isn't always something you feel. Sometimes, it's something other people feel for you until you can feel it for yourself again.

Karen:

Tears formed in my eyes as I drove around the corner, seeing our friends lined up on the street. I was blown away by how many showed up. That's what true community does—it shows up not when it's convenient, but when it's necessary.

I saw clearly how God's love is expressed through people—through hands that hold signs, arms that give hugs, and voices that cheer even when the battle is far from over. They became hope incarnate, holding our faith in trust when we were too tired to carry it ourselves.

Chris:

The years that followed tested this community-held hope repeatedly. There were setbacks, complications, and moments when waiting for a kidney transplant felt unbearable. But through every valley, they remained constant.

My church family understood that hope requires maintenance. It needs to be tended by people who believe in your tomorrow even when you can't see past today. They prayed when I couldn't pray, believed when I couldn't believe, and held onto my future when I could only focus on surviving the present moment.

Karen became my North Star. She didn't just stand by me; she stepped into the darkness with me, carrying light when I couldn't see my own hand in front of my face. Her love wasn't the romantic kind celebrated in movies—it was the fierce, determined love of someone who refuses to let you disappear into despair.

Karen:

Those five years tested both of us in ways we never imagined. There were nights when I heard the desperation in his voice: "I don't know if I can keep doing this." Instead of trying to fix him or offer false reassurance, I learned to simply stay. To hold him. To remind him: "You're not done. You are still here. And I'm not going anywhere."

Our community echoed that same truth week after week, year after year, becoming a foundation beneath us when everything else felt like it was collapsing.

Chris:

Then, almost exactly five years after this journey began, the call came.

It was 10:31 p.m. on Saturday, April 5, 2025: "We have a kidney for you. Would you like it?"

After all the waiting, all the prayers, all the nights when hope felt impossible to grasp, my miracle had finally arrived. At 4:15am, we drove to the hospital and had a successful surgery a few hours later.

I named my new kidney Rocky—because this journey was a fight. Not just for life, but for hope. For joy. For meaning.

The gift came with a profound understanding of sacrifice. My kidney came from a deceased donor—someone whose family transformed their deepest grief into someone else's greatest hope. This stranger's sacrifice became my salvation, a truth that carries both profound gratitude and weighty responsibility.

Together:

As we write this, months into new life with Rocky, we're struck by how hope revealed itself through this entire journey. It wasn't the optimistic feeling we had expected, but something far more powerful: the lived experience of being loved by a community that refused to let us face the darkness alone.

Hope, we learned, is not a solo endeavor. It's a community project, fueled by the love of people who choose to believe in your story's continuation even when you can't see the next chapter. It's found in the friend who shows up with a meal, the spouse who researches kidney-friendly recipes, the church family that lines your street with signs, and the stranger whose final act of generosity becomes your new beginning.

If you're walking through something heavy right now—if you're in your own valley—you don't have to do it alone. Hope doesn't always come from within. Sometimes it comes from those around you. From a community that loves you in word and action. From people willing to hold your hope in trust until you're strong enough to carry it again.

This is the power of hope through community: it transforms individual suffering into collective strength, personal despair into shared purpose, and one person's valley into a testimony that lights the way for others. Hope isn't just something we feel—it's something we do for each other, one hug, one prayer, one act of love at a time.

Hope isn't about believing everything will be okay. It's about believing you won't face whatever comes next alone. And in that truth—in the unshakeable foundation of faith, love, and community—there is more than enough light to keep walking, even through the darkest valley.

We made it through the valley together. And together, we discovered that hope—anchored in faith, built by love, and carried by community—truly is unshakeable.

About the Authors:

Christopher Laos

Christopher Laos is a resilient and community-focused individual from the Bay Area, California. Despite being diagnosed with kidney disease over five years ago, Christopher has faced his health challenges with strength, supported by his family and faith. After enduring years of dialysis, he received a life-saving kidney transplant in April 2025, marking a fresh chapter in his life. Now living in Oakland with his wife, Karen, and their two cats, Christopher continues to inspire others with his story of hope, perseverance, and gratitude, while also advocating for organ donation and serving his local church community.

Karen Laos

Karen Laos is a communication expert and confidence coach dedicated to helping women overcome self-doubt and find their voices in professional and personal spaces. With over 25 years of experience advising C-suite executives and speaking at renowned organizations such as Google, Starbucks, and NASA, Karen empowers women to confidently speak up, negotiate for what they deserve, and advance in their careers. As the author of *Trust Your Own Voice: Growing Your Influence Through*

Confident Communication and host of the *Ignite Your Confidence* podcast, she shares actionable strategies to build influence and foster trust.

Scan the QR Code to Learn More:

Want to sound more confident? Many of us use words by habit that steal our credibility. Do you unknowingly use these common authority killers in your speech? Find out and learn what to say instead.

To Move in the Freeze

By Katherine Singer

Waves lap the shoreline, their origin formed from a frozen place. They are a special kind of movement stemming from the hardness of ice. I dip my fingers into the chilly flow. I come here often to this lake to get away from the fast pace and demands of daily life, to reconnect with myself and my Maker. Something about this place requires that you leave your stress at the turn in the road where the cell service quits and focus on nothing more than this expansiveness of water, hemmed in by mountains that call the heart upward.

Like many in the beautiful state of Alaska where I live, this lake is an outflow of a massive glacier. There is nothing so inspiringly breathtaking or awe-inducing as walking up close to one of these walls of ice—layers upon layers of snow and cold built up over years of time—and hearing the glacier groan as it moves ever so slightly. Or to stand far away and watch it release a part of itself as tons of falling weight crash down with a mighty, roaring force. From these behemoths come the land of hundreds of lakes that dot the landscape, ice-melt providing water for all things living. This massive lake is no different, stretching down the valley more than twelve miles before it meets its partner body of water which will take it eventually into the ocean.

The metaphor is not lost on me: that something so solid and cold as a glacier could birth a moving thing that so many would depend on and which would bring forth new life from its most frozen and hard place. Much like me. Like my story. Like my heart. Like my life. I sit in the silence of the otherwise still landscape as the rhythmic *splash . . . splash . . . splash* continues to crash on the rocky beach where I'm sitting on a log of driftwood, silently breathing deep and reflecting. This whole scene so much represents where I've been: at times the frozen thing and at others, the moving one. And if there's one lesson my journey has taught me, it's that one always has a choice whether they will let their hard, massive thing create something redemptive and fresh or if they will stay frozen forever.

2019-2021 were some of the hardest years of my life—and not even because of all of the global turmoil that was happening. I often refer to this period as the second darkest time I've ever experienced . . . the first being over a decade earlier due to a loved one's health condition. In this more recent two-year span, my family and I lost over twenty-five people we know. One Saturday in particular, I attended two memorial services back-to-back, held just a couple miles away from each other. Some passed from terminal illness or cancer, one from a car accident, my childhood Sunday School teacher took his life after an extended physical and mental battle, my only remaining grandma died and, perhaps the hardest of them all, I received word that I'd lost one of my dearest friends suddenly at the age of thirty-one from a heart attack.

As I'm writing this, it's about to be the six-year anniversary of that evening when my whole world turned upside down and I had to accept that someone who had been for several years like the older brother I never had was gone forever. It happened so suddenly, too. A sergeant in the Marine Corps for over ten years, he had survived multiple deployments and a serious injury and had been rebuilding his life after leaving the military, intent on a legal career that would continue his passion for serving people. The tears flowed as I read the obituary and stared at his picture. It seemed so hard to believe. Yet, in that moment, I also felt like I was being led on a strange journey of meaning—that the darkness of my grief also held the potential to help me see something new that I would otherwise have missed. The pain felt overwhelming, but something also seemed to be telling me this was a hidden gift, if only I would lean into it.

In the wake of both the loss of my close friend and the many other deaths and suffering that seemed to be happening around me in that season, I made a decision to turn my face into the darkness. Years before, in the first really dark season of my life, I didn't have the tools to know how to meet suffering with grace, so I walked through it closed off to love and life, allowing the pain to harden me more and more . . . just like the layers of that glacier. I didn't understand until several years later that how you let your suffering shape you will determine whether you remain frozen in time or move forward like the tide of the lake.

I had learned my lesson from that first dark period, and I didn't want to make the same mistake again. I knew I needed to keep my soul open to the Light, however dim it felt. At times, as I battled the depression, the numbness, the isolation that is grief, that light often felt like a faint glimmer. The darkness felt and appeared far more prevalent. Yet, during that season that stretched on for months with no sign of relief, I discovered "what a friend we have in Jesus, all our sins and griefs to bear."

It wasn't through the tranquility of a life without pain that I learned what hope meant; rather, it was in the crashing waves of the storm that I heard that whisper of a Voice say, "I'm here, and I'll make sure that you're okay." It was in embracing the wave that cast me over and over against the Rock of Ages that I finally understood what it meant to believe and experience that God is a shelter for the oppressed (Psalm 9:9). When treading water is all you can do and the waves just keep washing you hard against the rock, the hiding place of God's care is the safest place you can be.

Even though I'd grown up knowing about God, it wasn't until I had to see God in the dark that I grasped the truth of what I now consider to be my life verse: "I am the light of the world. Whoever follows me will not walk in darkness, but will have the light of life" (John 8:12). For years I'd thought this meant my life would be free of trouble. I figured out quite quickly that wasn't true at all. The dark nights of the soul come for all of us at different times. A life without pain is actually no life at all.

The difference is that when you trust God's hold on you in the darkness, His loving compassion in the pain, you find out that there is always hope. Maybe it's only in the tiniest amount some days but, if you continue to trust that moving current in the middle of the frozenness that is your heart, you will come out the other side. Because the moment you lose hope and choose to let yourself stay stuck forever in the pain of what you've lost, you ultimately lose everything. Healing comes when you're willing to put your trust in a bigger purpose than what you currently see.

The last couple of years, I've been able to see where the river-movement has been leading. I've been a witness to how God has used the overwhelming grief of that dark season to birth new things that I otherwise never would have dreamed. Even in the most painful losses we walk through, I can attest to the fact that God knows what He's doing. It may feel like you've been absolutely wrung out, you've cried all the tears you can, and it feels like it will never get better. But there is "another side" to the storm.

There is that still-calm that comes from knowing that you are held in the storm by the same Hands who hold the world together. You are never out of His sight and always on His mind. He is the anchor that you can count on when everything in your life falls apart. As long as you are with Him, you will survive. You may still have the scars to prove what you went through, but you will be amazed as He takes the broken pieces and turns them into something beautiful.

I gaze up at the mountains around as the waves still lap at the shore and I think of the words of the Psalmist-King in Psalm 121 when he answered his own question: "I lift my eyes to the mountains—where does my help come from? My help comes from the Lord, the Maker of heaven and earth. He will not let your foot slip—he who watches over you will not slumber . . . The Lord will keep you from all harm—he will watch over your life; the Lord will watch over your coming and going both now and forevermore."

The hard places that, in past seasons, felt like they might keep me in their chilling grip forever have given way to a moving current of grace that bears me along, and now seeds hope not just for me but many more. And strangely, the waves which once felt like they would swallow me whole now serve as an assuring reminder to me that, whatever future storms I may encounter, I will be kept safe.

About the Author:

Katherine Singer is a writer who calls the beautiful state of Alaska her lifelong home. She is a trauma survivor and mental wellness advocate. She also has a weekly blog and hosts her own podcast. In her spare time, she loves being outdoors, staying active in her community, spending time with family and friends, and appreciating the wonder of being alive to the gift of life and love.

Scan the QR Code to Learn More:

If you are interested in exploring and elevating your own mental health or would like to learn more about Katherine's story, you can do so by visiting her website. You will find resources such as access to her weekly blog and podcast as well as ways to follow her on social media and contact her directly.

Unbreakable by Design

By Laura Spaulding

I was just nineteen when the United States military decided I wasn't good enough to serve my country. Not because I failed a test, not because I lacked discipline, courage, or loyalty—but because of who I loved. In 1994, "Don't Ask, Don't Tell" wasn't just policy—it was a loaded gun pointed at anyone who dared to live honestly. Just a couple of months prior they had given me an award, and now they gave me a discharge. I thought I was safe under the "Don't Ask, Don't Tell" policy, but I couldn't have been more wrong.

I joined the Army for two reasons. One, the only way out of my predicament was to get an education. The second reason was because I had nowhere to go. My parents kicked me out of their house for the same reason the Army did. As a matter of fact, I was pressured by my fellow soldiers to contact them for help. I put my pride aside and made the call home. I hadn't spoken to them in several months. My mother answered the phone and asked why I needed a lawyer. I told her they wanted to discharge me for being gay. She asked if that was true. I admitted it was. She responded, "Then you f***ing deserve it," and hung up.

Now I was homeless, broke, and had nowhere to go. I made $430 a month in the Army. Hardly a livable wage in the civilian world. I've replayed that moment in my mind more times than I can count. It didn't break me; it fueled me. I knew my success would be the best revenge.

I could have folded. Plenty of people would have. And honestly, maybe a piece of me did—for a minute—because I was nineteen, scared, and convinced the world hated me. I remember prior to enlisting I stayed with my friend and her family in their tiny two-bedroom townhome. They fed me and allowed me to share their home until I graduated high school. I was desperate for a sign. A way out of what seemed like a dead end. I had thought the military was my only choice.

I clawed my way into law enforcement—ironic, I suppose, to wear a badge after the uniform had rejected me. But policing was the one place I was up for the challenge. It was both a physical and mental challenge. It was another male-dominated industry, but I had something to prove. My determination to succeed anchored me. I spent seven years in the field. Patrol. Undercover vice. Narcotics. Dangerous work. Work that hardened my shell and sharpened my instincts.

I remember my first undercover buy. Sweating bullets in the beat-up pickup truck, praying the dealer wouldn't make us out as cops. I was given the option of wearing a wire or wearing a gun. I chose neither. I knew if either was discovered I would be killed so I chose to take my chances with my physical abilities. The adrenaline, the fear, the rush—all for a single bust that never even made the local paper. But for me, it was proof: I could handle anything. I could be the calm in the chaos.

But the real lesson came after the crime scene tape came down. I'd stand there, watching the families arrive—eyes hollow, hands trembling. The police would pack up the evidence bags. The medical examiner would leave. And then . . . nothing. No one cleaned up the blood. No one swept away the horror. It hit me: *Someone has to deal with what's left behind.*

In 2005, I decided that someone would be me. I had no money. No investors. No fancy marketing plan. Just a paid off SUV, and a stubborn belief that there had to be a better way to help people at their worst moments. I was tired of being poor, facing the glass ceiling, and living paycheck to paycheck. I had no money for marketing, so I knocked on funeral home doors on my days off. I sat in the lobbies of property managers' offices until they'd listen to my pitch. I offered a service nobody wanted to talk about—until they needed it desperately.

I still remember my first big cleanup—a double homicide on Christmas Day. Two family members got into an argument and shot each other. Right in front of the rest of the family. When I got there I saw a lot of blood. It was pooling and coagulating. It took me two days to clean it up by myself. But when the family came in, I saw the relief in their eyes. They didn't have to face that room. I did it for them. And in that moment, I knew: *This is what I was meant to do.*

But even with a business that mattered, bills didn't care about purpose. Equipment costs money. PPE costs money. Advertising costs money. I needed capital, fast. I went to four banks to get a business loan. They all turned me down. No one believed in my idea. I was depressed but determined. I had to figure out a way. I decided to ask for a home equity loan to replace the windows on my house. The bank gave me $15,000. The lie worked. It wasn't a lot of money but I could make it work.

So, I got scrappy. I taught myself real estate by devouring books, attending free seminars, and watching grainy YouTube videos at 2 a.m. when I should've been sleeping. I learned how to wholesale houses—contract, flip, repeat.

I still remember the first deal that hit. A mother of a hoarder called me to clean up her daughter's condo. The condo was in terrible shape. The hoarder was a raging alcoholic. The condo had mountains of vodka bottles everywhere. I decided to try my luck, and I mentioned I would buy the condo instead of cleaning it. I was terrified but made an offer of $5000. They accepted. I hired a handyman, and we redid the condo for $18,500. I later sold it for $65,000.

That first year, I did deal after deal. I offered to buy every crime scene house I was asked to come clean up. My first year I made $275,000—all from the leads that called me to clean up. Every dime I made in real estate went right back into my company. It was fuel for my fire.

By 2016, I was exhausted but proud. My company was thriving. I was getting calls from across the country: "Laura, how do I do what you do?" So I did what I thought was the next right step— I franchised.

On paper, it was a dream. Seventy-five locations in eight years. National recognition. Entrepreneur Magazine listed us as the top crime scene cleaning franchise. Inc. 5000 ranked us for 603% growth. People called me a self-made success story.

But behind the headlines was a bitter truth: success attracts sharks. Some of my franchisees were incredible, hard-working, heart-driven people. But most were vultures. They stole my proprietary systems. They siphoned my leads. They broke their contracts and competed against me in secret. I learned the hard way that not everyone who says they're loyal is.

I fought legal battles that drained my bank account and my spirit. I remember sitting in my office, wondering why I hadn't just stayed small. Why I'd trusted people with the thing I'd bled to build. But even then, I refused to give up.

When the dust settled, I decided to rebuild on my own terms. No more franchises. No more middlemen. Just my corporate location in Tampa, Florida—the original heartbeat of it all—and a new venture: mortuary transport. I bought an existing company, rebranded it as Bay to Bay Mortuary Transport, and brought the same compassion and discipline to this overlooked corner of the death care industry.

I made a promise to myself: *Never again will I hand the keys to my empire to people who haven't earned them.*

Now, I also run my Crime Scene Cleaning Academy. I coach the next wave of gritty, hungry entrepreneurs who want what I built—but faster, cleaner, smarter. I give them what no one gave me: the roadmap. The templates. The real numbers. The truth.

Sometimes people ask me if I'd erase my past if I could. If I'd want to be that nineteen-year-old kid who wasn't kicked out of the military. Who had loving parents. Who didn't have to fight for every inch of ground.

The answer is no.

Being rejected for who I am gave me the defiance to carve my own path. Being homeless gave me the hunger to never need a safety net. Getting stabbed in the back by people I trusted taught me how to protect what's mine.

I was never broken. I was just being forged. I was being made unshakeable.

If you're reading this, maybe you're at your own stormy rock bottom. Maybe you're tired of being told who you can be. Maybe you're holding your last twenty-dollar bill in your car, wondering if this world has a place for you.

It does.

You don't have to ask for permission to build your own table. You don't have to let anyone else define what success looks like for you. I didn't. And trust me—if a gay kid thrown out by the military and her own family can do it, you can too.

You see, unshakeable women aren't born. We're built. One failure, one betrayal, one heartbreak at a time.

So when they say you can't—build anyway. Brick by brick. When they slam the door—break through the wall. When they tell you you're too much, too different, too loud—smile, and keep going.

I made my own table. And I'm pulling up a chair for you, too.

This is what it means to be Unbreakable by Design.

About the Author:

Laura Spaulding is the founder of Spaulding Decon, a leading decontamination company in the United States. After 7 years in law enforcement and serving in the military Laura Spaulding started Spaulding Decon as a one woman show. In 2016 she franchised the company and had 75 locations across the country during the 9-year period. Featured in The Wall Street Journal, Inc Magazine, and Entrepreneur magazine she has become a featured expert in growing a dirty business. In 2020, Laura took the company to a 608% growth to make the Inc 5000 list at #784. Laura earned her spot on the Entrepreneur Franchise 500 list in less than 4 years of franchising. Laura created and produced the popular YouTube series Crime Scene Cleaning. With over 100 million views Spaulding Decon has become a household name and the go to for their services. Laura has scaled her business into owning over $10 million in real estate, and she owns several companies that are vertically integrated with one another.

Scan the QR Code to Learn More:

If this message stirred something in you, you're not alone—and you're just getting started. To learn how to start your own crime scene cleaning company with Laura's help go here:

My Unbreakable Journey of Passion & Purpose

By Megan DiMartino

I'm a New York girl deep in the heart of Texas—with a creative spirit, a servant's heart, and a relentless desire to mentor others.

For as long as I can remember, I've been driven by my creative passion. As a little girl, I was always creating something—whether it was fashioning a new dress for my doll or plotting the next adventure with my friends. That creative spark has never left me. It simply evolved.

My life's purpose? To help others discover their own dreams and walk confidently toward them—to see what's possible, not just what is.

But purpose isn't always paved with ease. Mine has been a journey marked by determination, heartbreak, reinvention, and above all—God's supernatural grace.

After two decades of building a career in national sales and marketing within the fashion and beauty industries, something stirred inside me. I had a vision that wouldn't leave me alone—a calling to create something revolutionary in skincare. It wasn't just about beauty; it was about transformation.

As a Baby Boomer, I watched my generation shift. We were no longer dancing in the summer of love—we were aging. But we didn't want to lose that vitality. I searched for products that offered real results, ones that didn't just mask aging but actively supported the skin's renewal. They didn't exist.

So, I made them.

In 1992, I launched Glycolique—one of the first professional-grade glycolic acid skincare lines. My mission was to empower salons, especially those focused on hair care, to expand into skin care and elevate their business model. It was bold. Unconventional. And ahead of its time.

But I soon learned that every new frontier comes with resistance and challenges.

Within three years, Glycolique gained national traction. I poured everything I had into it—my finances, my energy, my heart. But the momentum revealed a painful truth: I was undercapitalized.

Then came the offer. The manufacturer of my products approached me to purchase Glycolique. At first, I declined. But the pressures of growth and limited funds began to weigh heavily. Eventually, I accepted their offer with a one-year contract to continue building the brand while under their umbrella.

I intended to relaunch an even more expansive line after the year ended.

But then—everything changed.

The company that acquired Glycolique was itself acquired by a much larger entity. They didn't want the line. They offered me the chance to buy it back, and I did—signing a one-year buy-back agreement. I was elated. I was ready to reclaim my "baby."

But just as I was about to move the inventory into a new warehouse, the unthinkable happened.

They broke the agreement—a hostile takeover. They locked me out and refused to honor the contract, even after I had fulfilled my end of the bargain.

I was devastated. Everything I'd fought for was ripped away. My attorney urged me to sue—but something deeper within me whispered, *"No."*

Instead, I fell to my knees.

I cried out to God. In that moment of total surrender, I asked for a word. I needed divine direction in a situation no human logic could untangle. He led me to Psalm 37—a promise of justice, peace, and divine vindication.

And then, the miracle came.

My attorney's old law school roommate was now general counsel for the very company that had hijacked my dream. My story reached his ears, and he called my attorney, asking, "What does she want?"

"I want my money back," I said, with the quiet certainty of someone who knew Heaven had just intervened.

Within *one day*, the full amount was returned. A miracle, yes. But also—a new beginning.

Though I was relieved, the question still loomed: *Now what?*

My chemists, my team, even my attorney—all looked to me. *What will you do next, Megan?* I didn't have an answer. But I knew who did.

So I fasted. I prayed. I silenced the noise of the world and leaned into the still, small voice of the Holy Spirit. I cried out, "Lord, not my will, but Yours."

Then, like a whisper from Heaven, I felt drawn to a little prayer book I'd had since childhood. Inside was a small notecard. Typed across the front were the words:

> *"The call to new beginnings is ringing in the air. It is reaching through circumstances everywhere. Stand tall. Take the first step. The second and third steps will be revealed to you."*
> *—Psalm 37*

I had received my marching orders. That moment, in the quiet of my home office, became the catalyst for something new. A fire ignited—not just to rebuild, but to rebirth. Out of the ashes of Glycolique . . . came Novita.

Novita means *"new birth"* in Italian.

Novita . . . New Birth . . . New Life . . . Always Something New!

What a divine coincidence—or rather, *a God instance.*

Through Novita Spa Clinical Products, I expanded far beyond where I had started. It became more than just a skincare line. It became a full-service luxury day, medical & wellness spa, a community, and a mission to empower others to reclaim their confidence—inside and out.

I was no longer just creating products. I was helping people build their dreams, their businesses, and their belief in what's possible when you follow divine guidance over human doubt.

It's now been over twenty-eight years since I said yes to this journey. And if I had to do it all over again—every setback, every betrayal, every tearful night—I would. Because through it all, I wasn't walking alone.

The world may look at my story and see a strong woman. A business builder. A fighter.

But the truth?

What made me unbreakable wasn't *my* strength. It was *His* strength in me.

What sustained me in the dark was supernatural grace—the kind that holds you when your world shatters and guides you through decisions that feel impossible. I didn't get here because I knew all the answers. I got here because I kept listening. To the whispers. To the Word. To the Spirit of God who never once left my side.

My life's passion has always been to create. But my purpose—my true calling—has been to help others rise from their valleys, step into their dreams, and know they are never alone.

You may be reading this today facing your own setback. Maybe life has just pulled the rug from under you, and you don't know what's next.

Hear me when I say this:

"The call to new beginnings is ringing in the air."

It may look like ashes right now, but don't give up. The second and third step will be revealed once you take the first. Trust God. Trust that spark inside of you. Trust that nothing is wasted in His hands.

Believe in your vision. Trust your instincts. Your purpose will guide you—and your purpose is often revealed through your pain.

Choose to begin again. And when you do—never stop.

Every day, you and I have the opportunity to live a life that is unbreakable. Not because we are immune to pain—but because we serve a God who makes beauty from ashes.

"Trust in the Lord with all your heart,
and lean not on your own understanding;
in all your ways submit to Him,
and He will make your paths straight."
—Proverbs 3:5-6, NIV

Now go.
Create.
Shine.
And live your life . . . Unbreakable.

About the Author:

Megan DiMartino is a dynamic entrepreneur and mentor who has founded, scaled, and sold two award-winning seven-figure businesses in her impressive 30-year career. Since 1992, she launched successful skincare brands Glycolique and Novita Spa Clinicals, as well as the renowned Novita Spa and Medical Rejuvenation Clinic. Megan's book *Hope and Possibilities Just Over the Horizon: It's Never Too Early or Too Late to Create the Life of Your Dreams* became a #1 Amazon bestseller in four business categories in 2020. In 2022, she introduced Novita Beauty & Regenerative Wellness, focusing on innovative treatments like Stem Cell Therapy, IV Vitamin Infusions, and Red-Light Infrared Sauna Therapy. A TEDx speaker in 2024, Megan is committed to empowering others through her consulting, mentorship, and virtual course *PROPEL: Start, Scale and Sustain the Business and Life of Your Dreams*, offering entrepreneurs and individuals the tools to achieve their goals and unlock infinite possibilities.

Scan the QR Code to Learn More:

It's never too early or too late to create the life and legacy of your dreams.

There's Always a Way

By Ral West

Our greatest triumph was born from the depths of despair. I grew up in Seattle in an entrepreneurial family. My early childhood memories include my mother's favorite motto: "Where there's a will there's a way." I also witnessed my father facing challenge after challenge in his Alaska tourism business. Whatever the obstacle, he always found a solution, though sometimes a bit unorthodox. My parents gave me my foundational belief in the possibility of defying the odds, and having faith that things will work out for the best. This faith became my anchor. When I began my own entrepreneurial journey in 1981, I had no idea how well my anchor would serve me, and how often I would rely upon it when faced with turbulent waters.

In 1980 I moved from Seattle to Ketchikan, Alaska, to become Director of Marketing for a tour company. A year later I decided to move to Anchorage, where I started a marketing consulting business specializing in tourism.

It was there that I met John Hardwick, whose office was across the hall from mine. My first clients were tourism businesses located in Hawaii. Hawaii has long been the most popular destination for Alaskans. John saw me traveling to Hawaii for free on business trips and said, "I want free trips to Hawaii too!" He was in real estate, but he started asking me many questions about how products are distributed and marketed in the travel industry, persistently asking questions until he figured out a way to combine real estate with travel. He started by contracting with Alaskans who owned vacation rentals in Hawaii, becoming the rental agent for those properties.

After guiding him to create a more appealing vacation package including inter-island air and rental cars, I said, "You know, this is what I do for a living. You can't get my expertise for free." He responded, "Okay, I'll buy you dinner." Eight months later John and I were married, in July of 1983.

We had become a team, and the business he started grew. We were packaging Hawaii travel arrangements with Trans-Pacific air between Alaska and Hawaii. We bought blocks of seats from various air carriers operating direct flights between Anchorage and Honolulu. The business was thriving and our family was growing. Then suddenly, the Hawaii air carriers pulled out of the market, leaving no direct flights between Alaska and Hawaii. *We could not get our clients to Hawaii for their vacations.* It was a devastating blow to our young business!

Immediately our revenues dropped to zero. Without this critical component, we had no product to sell. We were losing money every day. We had a small staff, but without revenue, we could not meet payroll from operations. Even after cost-cutting, we were compelled to take cash advances on our personal credit cards to cover overhead. We didn't know how we could survive this catastrophic storm. We were facing an enormous challenge; our business was on the verge of sinking. We were desperate; we needed direct air service to Hawaii to save our business.

It was time to truly assess our direction and set a course for the future of our business. Should we close the business? We knew the people of Alaska wanted and needed a consistent, easy and economical way to get to their favorite and closest sun, sand, surf vacation destination, only five and a half hours from Anchorage. Without direct air service they would be required to take the much longer and more expensive route through Seattle. We also had a responsibility to our staff.

As we were agonizing over the decision facing us, I remembered my mother's motto: "Where there's a will, there's a way." We decided to forge ahead, committed to meeting the needs of Alaskans. We clung to our anchor, our faith that we would find a way to survive this storm, even though it seemed impossible.

We needed to find a way to fill the void of direct air service between Alaska and Hawaii, a service that had been available to Alaskans for many years, via one carrier or another. In our desperate search for options, John discovered that there was an air carrier based in Honolulu that was operating a series of summertime charter flights between Alaska and Japan. In-between those charter flights the empty jet would fly back to Honolulu, a dead-head in both directions. He contacted the air carrier and convinced them to charter that jet to us; we would sell the seats on the otherwise empty flights between Anchorage and Honolulu.

But there was a hitch. The carrier wanted us to guarantee the charter by putting up a letter of credit. We couldn't do that; our resources had been wiped out from covering our business' losses. In desperation, we turned to John's mother, a schoolteacher who had a retirement fund. She pledged her entire retirement fund as collateral for the required letter of credit.

John was a very good salesman, and that summer he became *extraordinary*. He was not going to lose his mother's retirement fund!

Most of our friends, people in the travel industry and even our CPA said, "You're crazy! Alaskans don't want to leave Alaska in the summer!" They were sure we were headed for disaster. I analyzed our historical sales numbers and confidently said, "We've sold this volume of seats at this time of year before. There is enough demand to fill these charter flights. We can do this." It was a gamble, a huge gamble, but a calculated one. And we did it; we filled every flight. We won!

That was the beginning of our company's rapid growth era; we began chartering more and more jets. We chartered wide body jets like DC10's and 767's. And the business kept growing and growing.

But that growth created another set of challenges for us. By this time I was devoting my full attention to our growing charter air business. We were guaranteeing the charters ourselves now, so we had everything at stake. John and I were the mom and pop, running every aspect of our business. We were up to our eyeballs juggling all the details and demands of the business. The business owned us.

Our young daughter often came to the office after school; she did her homework while we worked late. Our dinners were typically McDonald's and other fast foods, eaten in our office while we finished the day's work that was not able to be completed during business hours. It was a terrible lifestyle. We were stressed, exhausted and overwhelmed; we were overweight and out of shape. This was not healthy! We couldn't keep living this way. Our family was suffering, we were suffering, and so was our relationship.

We needed to learn how to do things differently. We needed to find a way to stop working *in* our business, and instead work *on* it. I went back to college to get a degree in organizational management. I studied organizational culture and total quality management. I was determined to immediately use what I learned in the operation of our business.

One of our early mentors was Robert Kiyosaki, before he became the author of *Rich Dad, Poor Dad*. We studied with him in the late 1980s in Anchorage. In 1994, we were on the Big Island in Hawaii at the same time he was there. Over lunch with Robert at his hotel, he advised, "You have to get these books: *The E-Myth* by Michael Gerber and *The Great Game of Business* by Jack Stack." That afternoon we went to the bookstore, got those books, and read them. Before we landed in Anchorage, we were determined to implement these new concepts to improve the way we operated our business.

Those two books spurred a revolution in the way we ran the business, from an operational perspective. We created systems, made sure that our team was empowered, and gave them the proper direction and guidance to do their jobs the right way. We developed job descriptions and Standard Operating Procedures for the entire operation. We measured and tracked our performance data, creating reports so the whole team would know how we were doing. We shared the business' financials with our team and taught them how to interpret the data.

We focused on developing our company's culture, too. Robert Kiyosaki taught us about the "fruit bowl theory of business." A bowl maintains its consistent shape; the fruit in the bowl can be in any combination or order. We guided our team with that philosophy. "As long as you stay within our guidelines, within the bowl, we'll support you." Our team was empowered, and they loved it, and in fact they thrived on it. We also operated with a win-win philosophy and made sure our team won when the company did well. We found that the more we were able to delegate to our team and let go of the need to do it all ourselves, the more freedom we enjoyed.

About five years after we read those books and implemented their concepts, we were able to hire two managers, a CFO and COO. That was a turning point for us. We were no longer required to work in the business. We bought our second home on Maui and a yacht; we started enjoying our lives! Those two managers used the foundation we had laid, and they grew the business to tens of millions in annual revenue. Twenty-five years after starting the business, we successfully exited Hawaiian Vacations by selling it to Alaska Airlines.

The journey from our first risky summer charter to our profitable exit was not all smooth seas. We were occasionally hit by rogue waves along the way. Through it all, working together as a synergistic team, we successfully navigated the stormy seas.

Life still throws a tsunami at us from time to time. However, our steadfast belief and faith that "*There's always a way!*" has been, and will continue to be, our anchor as we face life's storms.

About the Author:

Ral West is a Visionary Business Leader and Systemization Expert, who employs her 4+ decades of entrepreneurial experience and her passion for business in her newest endeavor: "Ral West Livin' The Dream". Ral teaches entrepreneurs how to be the owner rather than operator of their business, so they can have a successful business AND live the life they deserve. She has an online course and a Mastermind program. Ral and her husband have founded several businesses, one notably achieving 8 digits in annual revenue before being acquired by Alaska Airlines in 2008. Ral has invaluable experience in scaling businesses and mastering the art of effective systemization. Ral honed her business acumen with real life experience. She is a master at the practical implementation of business theories to create effective processes that transform businesses and multiply success. A respected figure in the tourism industry and multifamily real estate circles, Ral has been a guest speaker on numerous podcasts and has authored courses. Ral and her husband live in Alaska and Hawaii when they are not jet-setting on their worldwide travel adventures.

Scan the QR Code to Learn More:

Ral is offering a valuable FREE GIFT that will guide you to creating a business that allows you to live the life of your dreams. You don't have to work "for" your business; you can work ON it. Use this QR code or link to request your FREE GIFT from Ral West Livin' the Dream.

Built to Rise: Mantras Are Magical

By Renee Jefferson

"There's always someone who has it worse."

That was the phrase I clung to as a child, over and over again. It echoed in my mind every time life felt too heavy, too unfair. I used it like armor. When I was molested as a young girl. When I felt the coldness of a stepmother who never truly embraced me. When my biological mother walked away, abandoned me, and left a hole I didn't have words for. *There's always someone who has it worse*, I'd say to myself, like my struggle was a puddle while someone else was drowning in a storm.

"Things don't happen to you, they happen for you."

I didn't learn this until much later. Until years after the passing of my husband . . . .

I saw it coming.

Not in a clear, logical way but in the kind of knowing that comes from the soul. Throughout our relationship, I would have vivid premonitions and feelings I couldn't explain. My spirit knew long before my mind could accept it.

I got married in my mid-twenties. Our marriage wasn't perfect, but our bond was undeniably sacred. I say that with confidence because throughout our time together, I experienced a series of powerful premonitions and déjà vu moments that I couldn't explain, but I couldn't ignore either. There was a constant whisper deep inside me, telling me my husband would die at the age of thirty-six. The voice also told me I would end up back in my hometown in Ohio, raising two small children on my own.

At the time, it felt impossible. I only had one child then from a previous relationship whom was a teenager. I wasn't even pregnant. The idea seemed absurd. I'd try to silence it and push it out of my mind. But the whispers kept coming.

Eventually, we had our first daughter. And then, a few years later, I became pregnant again, this time with our son. Still, I didn't connect the dots. I was so busy mothering and working. But the premonitions grew louder, stronger. My husband was thirty-six.

One day, he asked me to take time off from work. He had a surprise planned. He wanted us to go to his hometown in South Carolina. He was organizing a baby shower for me and a birthday party for our daughter. I didn't take time off that day, but I planned to call in that Friday. Strangely, on Monday when I went to work, I packed up everything—my photos, my mug, my little keepsakes. I brought it all home without knowing why. Something in me just said take it.

That evening, as we were driving our daughters to dance class, I looked up at the sky. The clouds were low and white, and sunlight was piercing through in a beautiful, surreal way. I turned to him and said, "Look at the clouds." He glanced up, smiled, and said, "The pearly gates are open."

That night, he died of a massive heart attack while working the overnight shift.

I was at home, pregnant, and couldn't sleep. The baby inside me was moving like never before . . . flipping and turning wildly. I wasn't hungry or uncomfortable, but something felt off. I got up and walked to the kitchen. As soon as I stepped in, the phone rang. I froze. It was 1:40 a.m.

My husband never called me that late. He knew I didn't have a phone in the bedroom; he had taken it out earlier that day. When I picked up, a woman asked, "Is this Mrs. Jefferson?" I said yes. Her voice was somber. She told me there had been an emergency at my husband's job and that I needed to come to the hospital.

By the time I arrived, they told me he didn't make it.

I didn't cry. I didn't scream. I was numb, completely frozen in disbelief. The next morning, I had to do the unthinkable: send out an email to friends and family. I used the same chain my husband used just hours earlier to invite everyone to our baby shower. Except now, I was writing to tell them he had died during the night.

That Friday, the day he planned for us to celebrate, I still traveled to South Carolina. I drove down in a car with our children while his body was shipped in a casket by plane.

A few weeks later, I gave birth to our son. My husband had named him after him and my-father-in-law. Five days after our son's birth, my father-in-law died from a heart attack, just as my husband did. It was September 11, 2007. That number became my angel number, a sign of transformation, new beginnings, and a call to embrace my potential. My husband would always say it's essential to get the credentials to maximize your potential. This was another sign.

And just like the premonition had warned, I ended up back in Ohio. I moved into our new home on the same day as our wedding anniversary. My husband had $36 in his wallet when he died. He passed at the age of thirty-six exactly as I had seen it, again and again.

For a while, I was surviving, not living. I was grieving and didn't even realize how deeply depressed I had become. I withdrew from everything familiar. Formal religion no longer gave me comfort, but my connection to a higher power deepened in ways I hadn't imagined. My faith became personal. Intuitive. Divine.

I knew I had to carry on. I had to live for both of us. I had to master the art of living.

I began to travel. I said yes to life. To God. To growth. To surrender.

What I know now is this: nothing happens by accident. Every heartbreak, every premonition, every whisper was preparing me for a greater purpose.

Now I say, "Things don't happen *to* me, they happen *for* me."

That shift changed everything. I stopped seeing myself as a victim of life and started understanding that I was being refined not destroyed. Every hardship carved something deeper in me. Every loss opened up a new layer of compassion, of purpose. I started asking, "What is this teaching me?"

When I need a reminder to keep going, I turn to one last phrase that continues to carry me:

"This too shall pass."

Those words became my lifeline to get over the bumps of life, a quiet promise I clung to when the storms of life threatened to drown me. After losing my husband, giving birth while grieving, and navigating unimaginable loss, I didn't just need to survive, I needed something that could help me rebuild.

That's when real estate saved me and became a higher purpose in my life.

But it wasn't just a business venture. It became my therapy, my creative outlet, my form of healing. When everything in my world had collapsed, real estate gave me something to put back together. Through paint, flooring, drywall, and design, I didn't just renovate homes . . . I was rebuilding *myself*, piece by piece.

I learned quickly that when you're trying to do something good or when you're determined to be great, there will always be people who want to tear you down. But I didn't let that stop me. If anything, it fueled me.

Then came the opportunity that would stretch my faith and belief in myself further than ever before—my first ground-up development. I had no prior experience building new construction, but I had vision. And I had belief.

I remembered watching *Reading Rainbow* as a child with its theme song that always stuck with me: *"I can do anything . . . take a look, it's in a book."*

That line "*I can do anything*" became more than a lyric. It became a part of my DNA. I've always believed that if something is possible, I can do it! And when I saw that raw land with incredible views in a prime location, I knew I had to go for it.

It became my first multi-million dollar development, and I became the first black female developer in Cincinnati, Ohio.

What followed was a mix of triumph and turbulence. Doors opened, opportunities flowed in, but so did the drama. From the beginning, there were people ready to sue, sabotage, or scheme. Despite it all, I pushed forward. I got 90% of the project done . . . right to the finish line before I was forced to sell it prematurely to another developer to complete.

It was a devastating decision. One that broke my heart and tested everything I believed about myself.

The stress during that time was almost unbearable. But I didn't cry; I pivoted, and in the darkest moments, that same old phrase whispered its way back into my spirit:

"This too shall pass."

And it did. Because it always does.

I may have had to let go of the project, but I never let go of my purpose. And what I learned through that experience about resilience, about boundaries, about trust, and about faith became more valuable than anything I could have gained from the profit alone.

Because now I know "things don't happen *to* me, they happen *for* me." Every test, every challenge, every tear—it's all part of the making of something greater.

About the Author:

Renee Jefferson is an author, real estate developer, and investor with over 20 years of experience in redevelopment, new construction, and strategic investment. She has written two books and built a successful short-term rental business. As Principal Developer at Jefferson Legacy Developers, she leads impactful residential projects.

Renee is committed to legacy building, empowerment, and creating spaces that inspire and endure.

Scan the QR Code to Learn More:

Unshakeable isn't just a book...it's a testimony. A reminder that no matter what you've faced, you can rise. You can rebuild. You can live again.

If you've ever questioned your strength... If you've ever faced loss, abandonment, or uncertainty... If you've ever needed proof that purpose can rise from pain...

You Are the Storm—and the Anchor

by Robert Acosta

"There is no passion to be found in playing small—in settling for a life that is less than the one you are capable of living."
—Nelson Mandela

The car's back seat floor was cold, cramped, and suffocating. I couldn't tell whether my eyes were open or closed—the darkness was all-consuming either way. I could feel the cheap fabric of the mat under my cheek, could smell the mix of sweat and engine grease. My body was tense, but my mind was racing. I was in survival mode.

A few hours earlier, my wife and I were driving through Mexico City. It was nearly midnight when a random car swerved in front of ours and stopped abruptly. Two men approached, one on each side. I rolled down the window, instinctively. A gun appeared. I was ordered out of the car. My wife stayed inside while I was thrown into their vehicle. It was terrifying, like being swallowed by a nightmare while fully awake. I lost sight of her. That was the last time I saw her—for what felt like an eternity. My heart didn't race. It stopped.

They drove me around, stopping at several ATMs, demanding that I withdraw money. When they were done with me, they dropped me in the middle of nowhere. Somehow, I made it back home. And by some miracle, she was there, unharmed. Safe. Alive. Whole. But I was not the same.

That night, something irreversible happened. Not just trauma. Not just fear. It was a crack in the story I had been telling myself. A rupture in the illusion of the safe life I had so carefully constructed.

I wasn't truly alive. I was merely surviving a so-called "secure" life. A life I had been building carefully but unconsciously, never asking if it was mine. I started to call it the "small life"—a life shaped by the three F's: Fear, Fatigue, and Finances. Each one slowly suffocated my sense of possibility.

This night didn't just break me. It woke me up. I had faced a situation I did not choose. And I survived it—not just physically, but mentally. How? Because in the darkest moment, I realized: *I still had my mind.* And I could still choose my thoughts. That was my first glimpse of what would become my most powerful belief: *My anchor is my Thinking.* You don't rewrite your life in a single day—but you can start with a single decision.

After the kidnapping, the illusion of safety vanished. But I didn't immediately change jobs, cities, or careers. I simply started asking better questions:

- What am I pretending not to know?
- What do I truly want?
- Why am I still here—unfulfilled, yet comfortable?

The answers scared me more than that gun ever did. I was playing small. That was my Storm.

"Tough times don't last. Tough people do."
—Ben Platt

Over thirty years ago, I was a young executive in Mexico City—hard-working, ambitious, and steadily rising. But over time, I noticed a pattern around me: burnout, illness, family struggles, and financial anxiety were everywhere. Still, everyone kept going, hoping things would somehow improve. It took me twenty years to realize I was heading down the same path—sacrificing health, peace of mind, and purpose for a paycheck. I felt stuck, drained, and bound by expectations I never truly chose. Then one day, it hit me: I can't live like this anymore.

Life will, at some point, whisper a question: "Will you keep playing small—or will you rise and become the person your dreams are waiting for?" In my executive role, I was "successful." But I wasn't alive. It wasn't the work—it was the compromise. The smallness. I had become a prisoner of my own playbook. So I made a decision—not just to leave, but to *lead*. To take 100% responsibility for my results.

After facing a risky situation I hadn't chosen—and overcoming it by directing my thoughts and mindset—I realized it's not what happens to you that defines you, but what happens next, how you respond. That insight led me to seek out challenges intentionally, on my own terms. I chose to live what I call a **Big Life**—a life of bold goals and meaningful risks, rather than settling for safety or comfort. That became my reward: a life worthy of my potential.

My anchor in becoming unshakeable was my *thinking*—the ability to guide my mind with clarity and strength. And the skill that supported it was *courage*. Some call this combination of factors *resilience*. I believe we're all building resilience over time, often without realizing it. A deeper force seems to gather our experiences, refine them, and shape our inner strength—until the moment we need it most: when the storm hits.

"Life shrinks or expands in proportion to one's courage."
—Anaïs Nin

I didn't want to avoid storms anymore. I wanted to create the kinds of experiences that demanded my highest self. The kinds of experiences that required me to grow. And in some ways, I already had.

One moment in particular stood out, etched into memory like ice on skin–literally.

"If you don't take the first step, you'll always stay where you are," my guide said, as a blast of icy wind hit my face. I stood at the ice wall of a mid-sized Himalayan mountain called Imja-Tse, near Everest Base Camp, adjusting my harness and battling rising fear. I hesitated—no clear way forward, no safe way back. One final tug on my gear, and I drove my crampons into the ice. That first strike was forceful, almost defiant—breaking through the fear that had built up for hours.

Step by step, I climbed the icy wall—not to conquer the mountain, but to move with it. Each thud of my boots, my mind translated into applause urging me higher. Fear faded. In its place came a vision: me, at the summit, beside my Sherpa. They say the mind can't hold fear and belief at once. That day, I chose belief.

Just as I found my rhythm, my ice pick slipped. My body jolted—but before panic took over, a strong hand grabbed my elbow. My Sherpa smiled and said, "You are here." We were at the summit. Endless white peaks stretched around us. My fear had vanished, replaced by awe. That day, I learned this: Fear lasts only a few seconds—just like courage. What comes next depends entirely on your decision to keep going.

"There is more to us than we know. If we can be made to see it, perhaps for the rest of our lives we will be unwilling to settle for less."
—Kurt Hahn

In January 2009 I stood alone under a frozen bus shelter in Toronto—cold to the bone, unemployed, and unsure of what came next. It was one of the coldest mornings of the year, and I was in a city that still felt foreign. I couldn't help but wonder how my life had ended up hanging by a thread—again—this time due to a global crisis I hadn't caused and couldn't control. Then I remembered, back in Mexico City I had once built a "successful" life. I had a solid career and financial stability—but deep down, I was at war with myself. Success came at too high a cost.

In the corporate world I knew, climbing the ladder meant stepping over others, compromising values, and playing by rules that didn't feel right. Even entrepreneurship wasn't immune—it often meant tolerating corruption or becoming part of it. For years, I lived in that contradiction—comfortable, but restless. Deep down, I knew: if I stayed, I would slowly trade away the person I wanted to be.

That cold morning in Toronto, I decided enough was enough. I was done waiting for circumstances to change. I would be the one to change. I chose courage over comfort, growth over safety. That very day, I sat across from a VP of a global company who told me he admired the guts it took to come to Canada like this. In that moment, something shifted. Canada wouldn't just be a place to live—it would be where I expanded, where I rose.

When I officially moved to Toronto in 2011, I had no job, no clear roadmap—just the fire of that decision still burning in me. Slowly, step by step, I rebuilt. I landed roles in global companies—not by playing the old game, but by showing up with boldness and integrity. Not for who I was willing to be on paper, but for who I refused to stop being. That's when my Big Life began.

"You don't try because life is difficult.
Life is difficult because you don't try."
—Mel Robbins

It was an early summer morning in Toronto. I was training for a triathlon, cycling with my coach. The streets were quiet, the wind cool. Then, I hit the edge of the pavement. My front wheel twisted. I flew over the handlebars and landed hard on my right hip. The fracture was clean, sharp, and final. I wouldn't be racing anytime soon.

An hour later, I lay in a hospital bed—oddly, in the children's emergency ward. I don't know why. Above me, painted on the wall, were the words: *Every cloud has a silver lining*. At first, I was frustrated. Then, something deeper emerged. A knowing. You don't change your life by moving countries. You change your life by mastering your mind. I had changed countries. But to change my life, I had to change *me*.

"The one investment that always outperforms: the one you make in yourself."
—Darren Hardy

That injury became the pivot I needed. The pain became my platform. I chose, once again, to embrace a Big Life. I mustered the courage, left my executive life for good, and started my own coaching firm.

Today, I coach others to rise into their Big Lives. Not because I have all the answers—but because I had found mine. Because I've felt what it's like to be buried on the floor of a backseat—and to rise on purpose to the top of a mountain.

After facing storms—some I didn't choose, and others I walked into—I discovered one common success factor: the power of a strong mind. A strong mind doesn't predict the future. A strong mind endures it. Shapes it. Leads it. That was the key shift: from needing life to be easy—to becoming someone who could handle anything.

"Don't wish it were easier. Wish you were better."
—Jim Rohn

My storm is settling for a small life.
My anchor is my thinking.
My greatest skill is courage.
My superpower is choosing uncertainty.

The most powerful way to face whatever storm life throws at you—and to transform any challenge into a stepping stone toward a joyful, purposeful, Big Life—is to choose growth.

And growth isn't about climbing higher; it's about becoming stronger. It's about pursuing your Big Life with boldness and heart. It's about going where others won't—not for the thrill, but to honor your truth.

The circumstances I faced could have broken me. Instead, I chose for them to *build* me.

And now, I invite you:
Don't settle. Don't shrink. Don't delay.
The Big Life is already inside you.
Your move.

About the Author:

Robert Acosta is an Impact Life Coach, social entrepreneur, and athlete based in Toronto. Originally from Mexico City, he blends analytical expertise with a passion for growth. With decades of experience in human behavior and global brands, he now guides individuals and organizations to unlock purpose, courage, and high-impact results through his coaching practice, Full-Time Giver—empowering others to live fully, break limits, and build a Big Life.

Scan the QR Code to Learn More:

Feeling momentum? Let's talk. I'm offering a free Momentum Call (normally a paid service) to help you identify your top three challenges and create a plan to overcome them within the next 12 months. DM me "MOMENTUM" on LinkedIn to schedule.

From Chaos to Clarity: A Journey Through Clutter, Trauma, and Love

By Valerie Huard & JM Tetreault

I remember the moment I broke, not because something huge happened, but because I couldn't find a matching sock.

Standing in my hallway, surrounded by piles of laundry that had been there for days (or was it weeks?), I felt my chest tighten and my vision narrow. The sock in my hand, just a simple black sock, became impossibly heavy. My fingers trembled. The musty smell of unwashed clothes mixed with the stale air of a space I'd been avoiding. And then, without warning, I sank to the floor and sobbed.

Maybe you know this feeling. Maybe your breaking point isn't a sock, maybe it's unopened bills, unanswered emails, or a sink full of dishes that feels insurmountable. Maybe you, like me, present a polished version of yourself to the world while drowning in private chaos.

It wasn't about the sock. It was never about the sock.

It was about everything the sock represented: one more thing I couldn't manage, one more reminder that beneath my carefully-constructed professional exterior, my life was spiraling. The clutter around me wasn't just physical, it was the visible manifestation of emotional weight I'd been carrying for so long.

In that moment, crumpled on the floor among scattered clothes, I didn't know that this breaking point would become my turning point. I couldn't see how this collapse would eventually lead to the anchor that would steady me through every storm since.

You don't break when the big things fall, you break when the little things crack.

The relationship between my past trauma and present chaos wasn't something I understood immediately. Growing up, my grandfather had been a source of danger and abuse for as long as I could remember. Control became a precious commodity, something always just beyond my reach when he was around. I learned early that safety was fragile, that you had to manufacture protection through vigilance, through perfect behavior, through becoming invisible when necessary.

These were survival skills then. They became liabilities later.

If you've lived with a constant source of unpredictability or danger in your early years, you might recognize this pattern. Your nervous system, wired for protection from ongoing threats, doesn't easily distinguish between past and present dangers. What once kept you safe now keeps you stuck.

As an adult, I built a life that looked successful from the outside. I had credentials and achievements, a career that demanded respect. I became exceptionally good at compartmentalizing, at presenting a polished version of myself to the world. But behind closed doors, the fortress was crumbling.

Our home became the physical representation of my emotional state, overwhelmed, disorganized, filled with things I couldn't seem to process or release. Every surface held piles: mail I was afraid to open, clothes I no longer wore but couldn't part with, books half-read then abandoned, projects started with enthusiasm then left unfinished when perfectionism paralyzed me.

I tried to fix it, of course. I'd spend frantic weekends cleaning, organizing, purging. I bought storage solutions. I read books about minimalism. I created elaborate systems that would surely work this time.

They never did.

Because what if the clutter wasn't the cause . . . but the symptom?

The spiral accelerated gradually, then suddenly. Our home became a place where I felt exposed and ashamed. I stopped inviting people over. I made excuses. I lied.

"Our place is being painted." "We're in the middle of renovations." "Let's meet at the cafe instead."

Perhaps you've told similar lies. Perhaps you've felt the exhausting weight of maintaining a facade while your private world feels like it's falling apart.

The shame was corrosive. How could someone so competent professionally be so dysfunctional personally? The cognitive dissonance exhausted me. I spent energy maintaining the facade that could have gone toward healing.

The clutter became a physical barrier between me and the life I wanted. Bills went unpaid because I couldn't find them. Deadlines were missed. Opportunities slipped away. Simple tasks became monumental challenges. Finding clean clothes for work required archaeological excavation.

The voice in my head grew increasingly harsh: *You're a mess. You're broken. If people knew the truth, they'd be disgusted. You should be able to handle this.*

When everything around you feels chaotic, it's hard to hear your own voice, let alone trust it.

JM and I have shared our lives for nearly three decades, but there came a moment when he became more than my partner. He became my witness. And in that witnessing, I found my first anchor: *the transformative power of being truly seen without judgment.*

We'd been living together for years, but I'd become masterful at compartmentalizing even within our shared space. I'd create pockets of order when he was around, then retreat to my chaos when alone. But one day, the mask slipped completely.

"You don't have to explain," he said when I started making excuses about the state of our home. His eyes held something I couldn't identify at first. Not judgment, but recognition.

He understood that look, the weight of carrying invisible burdens while trying to appear functional.

JM didn't try to fix me. He didn't offer solutions or criticism disguised as help. Instead, he created space, physical and emotional, where I could begin to face what was really happening.

"Tell me about one thing," he'd say, pointing to a pile of papers I'd been avoiding for months. And he'd just listen as I unraveled the complex emotions tied to something as simple as unopened mail.

If you're reading this feeling isolated in your struggle, know this: sometimes what you need most is someone who sees the weight you're carrying and doesn't try to fix it, just helps you unpack it.

This became my anchor, not the relationship itself, but the radical experience of being witnessed with compassion. It taught me that healing doesn't happen in isolation, and that there's profound power in letting someone see you as you truly are.

The shift didn't happen in a single dramatic moment. It came in whispers, in small realizations that accumulated quietly.

One evening, sitting amid another pile of clothes I was trying to sort, I found myself frozen again. JM sat down next to me, our shoulders touching.

"What's happening right now?" he asked gently.

"I don't know what to keep and what to let go of," I said, but even as the words left my mouth, I knew they weren't just about the clothes.

"What if," JM suggested, "we start with just one thing that feels safe to release?"

That night, we created a new ritual. One item at a time. No pressure for perfection. A pause to notice what emotions arose. A moment to honor them. Then a conscious choice: keep or release.

Here's what I learned that might help you: *Start impossibly small.* Not with the whole room, but with one corner of one surface. Not with all your clothes, but with one piece you haven't worn in years. Not with perfection, but with compassion.

We created tiny islands of order that slowly expanded. Not because the space needed to be perfect, but because I needed to feel safe. JM helped me see that my brain, wired by earlier trauma, interpreted clutter as a threat, a constant reminder of chaos that kept me in survival mode. By creating predictability and small wins, we were retraining my nervous system to recognize safety.

The anchor of compassionate witnessing evolved into something I could give myself: self-compassion in the midst of mess. Instead of berating myself for the chaos, I learned to ask: "What does this clutter represent? What am I trying to avoid feeling?"

Letting go wasn't about the stuff. It was about believing I could handle what came after.

Clarity came in stages, like fog lifting gradually to reveal a landscape I'd forgotten existed.

The first revelation was understanding that my "organizational problem" was actually a trauma response. My brain had been so busy scanning for threats that it couldn't prioritize or process. The executive dysfunction wasn't laziness or character failure, it was neurobiology.

If you've ever felt broken because you can't seem to do what others do effortlessly, please hear this: *your struggles may be your nervous system's attempt to keep you safe, not evidence of your inadequacy.*

The second revelation came through connection. Sharing my story, first with JM, then with a therapist, then with trusted friends, I discovered I wasn't alone. The specifics varied, but the pattern was common: unresolved trauma manifesting as environmental chaos.

As my space began to reflect more order, my mind followed suit. I developed the capacity to sit with discomfort rather than avoid it. I learned to recognize when I was slipping into old patterns and created gentle ways to guide myself back.

Your anchor might be different from mine. Maybe it's therapy, movement, creativity, spirituality, or community. The key is recognizing that you need something outside yourself to help you weather the storm, and that asking for help isn't weakness, it's wisdom.

JM and I began documenting what worked, creating a framework based on neuroscience and compassion rather than willpower and shame. What began as my personal healing journey evolved into something we felt compelled to share, helping over 35,000 people who confirmed what we suspected: We were never alone in this. Most people just don't talk about it.

If this was possible for someone drowning in it all, it's possible for you, too.

Looking back at that woman sobbing on the floor over a sock, I feel immense tenderness. She wasn't broken. She was buried under expectations, under trauma responses that once protected her, under the physical manifestation of emotional weight she'd carried too long.

The journey from chaos to clarity wasn't linear. It still isn't. There are still days when old patterns resurface, when the pull toward disorder feels magnetic. The difference now is that I recognize these moments as information, not indictments of my worth. I have my anchor: the knowledge that I can be seen, accepted, and supported exactly as I am.

This isn't a story about perfect transformation. It's about finding solid ground amid the storm, about building capacity for the inevitable waves that come, about learning that being unshakeable doesn't mean never trembling. It means knowing you can steady yourself again.

If you see yourself in these words, here's what I want you to know:

- Your chaos isn't character failure. It might be your nervous system's way of coping.
- You don't have to fix everything at once. Start with one small, safe thing.
- Being seen and accepted as you are is a fundamental human need, not a luxury.
- Your anchor might be a person, a practice, a belief, or a community, but you need something to hold onto.
- Healing happens in relationship, not in isolation.

If your own space feels like a battlefield rather than a sanctuary, know this: *You're not broken. You're human.*

And what if this isn't your breaking point, but your turning point?

You don't have to do it alone. Find your witness. Find your anchor. Find your way back to yourself.

The storm will pass. But with the right anchor, you'll still be standing when it does.

About the Authors:

Jean-Michel (JM) Tetreault is a father, mentor, productivity expert, mindset coach, and retired senior military officer. Drawing from a background in strategic leadership and personal resilience, he empowers others to find clarity and overcome obstacles.

Valerie Huard is a trauma-informed wellness expert and bestselling author who helps individuals break free from clutter and reconnect with their inner anchor. With a background in occupational therapy and a lived journey through Complex PTSD, she co-founded DO Well® and the Doers Academy with JM Tetreault.

Together, they developed the DO Well Method—a holistic approach that blends emotional healing with practical action to empower individuals to move from overwhelm to lasting transformation. Co-authors of the international bestseller Put That Stuff Down, Valerie and JM are dedicated to helping people overcome mental clutter, anchor themselves in purpose, and create meaningful, sustainable growth.

Scan the QR Code to Learn More:

To support your journey, we've created a free Clarity Starter Kit—the same gentle starting point we wish we had when everything felt too heavy to carry. To get your kit please click above or scan the QR code.

Unshakeable: Anchored in Love

By Wendy M Watson

I was sitting in a pew at a church, there to support a friend who had just lost his uncle to an overdose. The sanctuary was heavy with silence and sorrow. Friends and family shuffled in, eyes red, shoulders slumped, hearts hollow.

As I sat listening to the sermons and stories, watching grief ripple across faces, my eyes settled on the widow—my friend's aunt. Her composure was brave, but the exhaustion in her spirit was louder than any words being spoken. And suddenly, I wasn't just witnessing her pain—I was living it.

In my mind, I saw myself standing where she was. I saw the quiet despair, the endless worry, the nights spent wondering if it would be "the last time." I saw myself presenting my own husband's future funeral—another life claimed by addiction.

And then, I realized—I wasn't just imagining it. I was being shown a possible future. A warning. A truth I didn't want to accept, but couldn't ignore.

You see, just days before, I had discovered that my husband had been "hiding" a cocaine addiction from me—for over four years. And what he hadn't realized, or couldn't admit, was that his "recovery" had simply turned into another addiction. He was now drinking half a gallon of whiskey every three days.

What was disguised as recovery was actually just a new spiral. And there I was, sitting in that pew, holding a mirror to someone else's heartbreak, seeing my own reflection staring back.

Surrounded by grief, I was shown a choice: I could stay, honor the vows I made "for better or for worse," slowly lose myself to the chaos and walk a path of constant stress, fear, and caretaking. I could stay, and in doing so, slowly dissolve my own future, one sleepless night at a time.

Or *I could choose me.*

I could choose my sanity, my spirit, my dreams, and my peace. I could walk away from a marriage that had already been broken by his choices. I could rewrite the story before it wrote itself into tragedy.

By choosing his addiction over our marriage, he had made the first choice. And I was now being asked to make mine.

That moment was my storm. But it was also the beginning of my anchoring.

I went home and did something ceremonial. I made a list of all the reasons I fell in love with him nine years earlier. I sat with that list in silence, reading each reason out loud to myself. And with each one, I felt the ache of distance. He was no longer that man. He hadn't been for a long time.

I cried.

Not the gentle, cinematic kind of crying. I wept with my whole body. My soul sobbed. It was the kind of pain that only comes when you realize a dream you've been fighting for has already died.

At thirty-six years old, I found myself staring at a heartbreak I'd known before. This wasn't my first time at the crossroads. I had already walked through divorce once—from someone who had emotionally and psychologically abused me, someone who had shattered my heart in different but equally devastating ways.

I'd survived betrayal. I'd picked up the pieces of my shattered heart once already. And now, ten years later, I was staring down the same dark tunnel. Another betrayal. Another goodbye. Another man who chose something else over the life we were building together.

I don't take marriage lightly. I never have. It's a sacred contract to me—one that I enter with full heart and full intention. And still, I found myself twice divorced, both times not by my own doing, not because I didn't try. But because *I had to survive.*

The road ahead looked terrifying. I was only three years into a new career. I had never lived alone. I didn't know if I could afford the house without him. We had a roommate—what would happen with that? I had no idea what the next month would look like, let alone the next year.

But I did know this: I couldn't stay in a story that wasn't mine anymore.

I did have a decision. I didn't need to know every step ahead. I only needed to take the next one.

I didn't need all the answers—I only needed one truth: *I had to love myself more than the unknowns.*

I had to love myself more than the vision I saw in that church. I had to trust myself, the version of me that had survived once before—and would do it again.

So I chose love.
I chose me.

During my divorce, I met someone unexpected. He was kind, safe, grounding. Twenty-five years my senior, also twice divorced, he became a source of comfort—a quiet harbor for my heart while I weathered the storm. He made me feel safe again. Not saved. Not dependent. No demands. No pressure. Just ... safe.

He reminded me that I was still a woman. That I was still desirable. That softness and affection still had a place in my life.

One night during pillow talk, I asked him if he would ever marry again.

"No," he said without hesitation. "I could never say 'I love you' to anyone but my daughter."

In that moment I realized that I wasn't willing to settle for less than what I knew I deserved. His honesty didn't hurt—it clarified. It showed me what I was no longer willing to accept.

I was too young to live the rest of my life untouched by that kind of love—romantic, intentional, affirming. I wanted and deserved to hear "I love you" not just in words, but in energy, in presence, in partnership. I didn't want to live my life as someone who had calloused their heart so much that love no longer flowed freely.

He taught me something beautiful in that moment: *I could not recreate his emptiness in my own life*. I could not become emotionally numb just because I had been broken. If I did, the storm would have won.

And I am not here to lose.

That moment became another anchor point for me—one that whispered, *Do not close your heart.*

It took time to heal—years, in fact. I had to unravel trauma I didn't know I was carrying. I had to relearn how to trust my intuition, how to soften again, how to open without fear of drowning.

I had to redefine love. Not as fairy tales and finish lines—but as truth. As presence. As something that begins, always, with myself.

And through it all, one truth kept me grounded and never wavered:

My anchor became love. Especially the love I have for myself.

Not just romantic love. Not just love for others. But a deep, unwavering, infinite love for myself. For my growth. For my truth. For my future.

No matter what storms come—divorce, career upheaval, pandemics, financial dips, friendships lost, homes changed—*I am anchored in love*. And that love makes me unshakeable.

What kept me steady was knowing that my worth isn't conditional on anyone's ability to see it.

What made me unshakeable was not how I avoided the storm—but how I held steady in the middle of it. Because I trusted the version of me that never stopped choosing love.

I don't wait for the world to calm before I steady myself.

I steady myself first—and that steadiness changes everything.

Storms will come. Life will shift. People will break my heart. But the love I anchor in—the infinite love for who I am, who I remember myself to be, and who I'm becoming—*holds me.*

That's what makes me unshakeable.

About the Author:

I'm Wendy Watson a 5th-generation entrepreneur, The Embodiment Architect, and the founder of The Love Legacy, Relationships That Scale, and Beyond the Blueprint frameworks.

I work with high-achieving men and women who are tired of living by someone else's rules. They've crushed goals, survived the hard stuff, built the empire—and yet still feel like something's off. They're ready to stop performing and start embodying. I won't clip your wings because I know you're ready to stop simply performing and start embodying.

Because I've lived it. Lost it. Rebuilt it. And chose love—again and again.

Scan the QR Code to Learn More:

Is it time to rethink a relationship in your life?

Take the free "Does This Relationship Still Fit?" quiz to get clear on whether your connection—whether with a person, a pattern, or a part of yourself—is aligned with the person you are now. Click above or scan the QR code to take the quiz and get your personalized next step.

Soul Refresh

By Wendy Wildt

I have bootstrapped my way through life. Fake it until you make it, proceed with positivity, just think your way into happy—I have tried all of these things. None of them worked for me. Maybe they do for some people, but I needed action behind all of these positive affirmations, and I found it during a year-long program with Tony Robbins.

My life changed when I decided on a soul refresh—really digging deep into what I love, what matters most to me, and how to actually get there.

My soul refresh this year is simple—lose weight, save money in my 401K, and pay off any old debt that is not serving me. It has been an incredible time of examining choices, determining outcomes, and charging forward to solutions. All of the time spent with Tony Robbins and then applying his concepts have sincerely paid off.

In 2022 I took a hard look at my life and realized it was not heading in the direction of my dreams. I talked to a dear friend at lunch, completely unloaded on him about not wanting to live my life as a victim, and signed up for a free weekend course in Dallas that set me on a new path forward in life.

That course was a total leap of faith—I signed up without knowing much other than my friend saying, you need to attend and I promise it will be good for you. It was free and I had a weekend available, so I signed up! The course in Dallas, Texas—Next Level Experience (NLE)—set me on a new path in life. That fall I attended my first Tony Robbins event, Unleash the Power Within. This event changed me as I came to a place where I started to believe that I could change my life. In 2023, I spent the bulk of my vacation time attending three additional Tony Robbins events followed by making serious changes. That year I hired two coaches and prayed my heart out for an upgrade.

My upgrade happened, and it sincerely put an anchor in my life.

Let me give you a few examples of how my life upgraded and my soul refreshed after going through Next Level Experience and the Tony Robbins programs. I have a book, *Buckets*, published on Amazon.com which was a ten-year journey for me. This book, which came together over multiple years, was in my dreams, part of my journals. I have multiple copies of the same story written in four places. It would not stop coming to me, and I am grateful as it took that for me to believe in the vision. Some of you may just need one sign, but I needed four!

What is your dream? What do you have written in four journals or perhaps tucked away in a closet? What did you share with your sister only once or told your best friend in secret asking her to take it to the grave? What if this is one of the unique gifts you're meant to share with the world?

Saying yes to a soul refresh is a game-changing experience, so let me encourage you to say yes! I said yes to a coach after Next Level. I said yes to sharing my dream at a conference in front of a successful book editor, and I said yes to showing two of my closest friends my chicken scratch book on paper and having them pray over me and the book. I said yes to people and then I started investing in others. I said yes to buying a painting from an NLE conference, yes to supporting a dear friend on her journey to public speaking, and yes to prayer with a group of women once a week for over a year.

What is your yes? What is your dream? What do you have tucked away in the back of your heart that your soul is asking you to give to the world, but you are too scared to go there?

How can you let the dream you have be sticky this year? What if your imagination really does have traction and there is a future for what is in your heart. I think this is the magic in life— letting our heart sing to us and share its voice. My heart sang for ten years about *Buckets* but it took a free conference, a group of women praying with me, a coach (thank you Robin McCoy), and a successful editor to get me there.

I am living proof that you can change no matter your age. If you want to be unshakeable, now is the time. For some straightforward and practical tips, here are the three steps I recommend taking to start making changes today.

1. Try the fifteen-minute trick. In Zoe Chance's book *Influence Is Your Superpower*, she talks about our alligator brain and how it's tricky to figure out. While reading this book, I started using the fifteen-minute trick that changed my life. You see, I have always wanted a clean home—you know, like the designer homes you tour around the Thanksgiving holiday that don't have a spot of dust anywhere! I could not ever get myself there. While reading the book, I started setting my microwave timer for fifteen minutes and began cleaning. Here is what changed—my home started to look cleaner, smell better, have less paper lying around, and when I walked into the home, I felt happy that it looked put together. For me, it's not about the size of the home or the things in it; it's about how I feel when I walk in after a long day. Is it clean? Does it smell nice (even if you have an animal like I do—I go to great efforts to keep it smelling good!)?

2. Find people you can run with. This will change over time, but I have a group of people that I can run with and it makes a big difference in my life. Some people I talk to once a week, some people I speak with daily, and I have a group of friends I see on a regular basis who really help me get unstuck when I am bogged down. Having friends who will listen, give advice, or perhaps just be supportive makes life a better journey.

3. Most importantly, figure out a way to anchor yourself every single day. My go-to right now is Tony Robbins free priming exercise and Hal Eldrod's Morning Miracle. Through morning meditation, grounding, and journaling, I anchor myself, and it has helped me continue down this path of progress.

If my story resonated with you, let's get social! I'd love to hear your story and share a free exercise I use for fifteen minutes to change. I'd love to hear what your soul is singing to you and how your heart wants to bring dreams to life.

About the Author:

Wendy is a dynamic and well connected account director who excels at helping companies solve business challenges across finance, supply chain and tax. She has deep experience working with CFO's and the c-Suite leaders and bring and impressive background of insight, heart, energy to every conversation. Wendy graduated from Greenville University with a follow up marketing certificate from UCSD during the global pandemic. Wendy has learned the grace to give compassion to herself and others through spiritual, emotional and mental changes. Her love for personal and professional growth is infectious. If her writing encouraged you, connect with Wendy & get social!

Scan the QR Code to Learn More:

As a career consultant at the Big 4 with prior Fortune 500 company experience join Wendy as she talks about the steps to keep your white collar job, future proof your career with AI and take the steps YOU need to weather the tech changes ahead.

Unshakeable: The Anchors that Ground Me

By Yvonne Pire

There are seasons in life when everything hits at once. Dreams feel out of reach. Relationships start to slip away. The strong face you wear begins to crack, and you wonder how you'll hold it all together.

I recently found myself in one of those seasons. Professionally, I was navigating the challenges of building a new business in a tough market. Personally, I was working through heartbreak. It all felt heavy, and I could feel myself starting to disconnect.

So, I stepped outside. I felt the sun hit my face and the wind move around me. I walked barefoot, letting the ground steady me as I collected rocks, something I've always loved doing. Smooth or jagged, rocks have all been shaped by time and pressure—just like me. Their weight grounds me and reminds me what's real. They're solid. Steady. When life feels shaky, I find my footing in their quiet strength.

They remind me to come back to myself, to ask three questions that have become my anchors:

- Am I being true to myself and others?
- Am I creating connections that support growth?
- Am I aligning with my vision?

I didn't find these questions in a book or a course. I found them in pain, in healing, in rebuilding after each storm. Every time I lost myself, these questions helped me find my way back.

The truth is, I didn't start life anchored. I started life pretending.

Some of my earliest memories are of lying still in my bed, wide-eyed in the dark, heart racing, waiting for the night to be over. My mom worked the late shift, and we kids were at home with the dad who should have protected us but instead did the opposite. I didn't have the words to name what was happening, but I knew how it made me feel. Ashamed. Confused. Frozen.

From the age of five to ten, this nightmare persisted. I learned to disconnect from my body. I smiled during the day even though I had suffered through the night. On the outside, I looked like a happy child. But inside, something had quietly broken.

That was the first time I lost touch with my truth. Not because I wanted to, but because I had to.

What saved me back then was my imagination. I would close my eyes and visualize a different life—one where I was safe and loved, where I felt true connection and joy. I didn't realize it then, but that vision became my lifeline.

After our young mom left our dad and she found out the truth about the abuse I had suffered, she unraveled. I'll never forget that horrible evening when she almost killed herself. No one explained what was happening, but I remember the confusion, the fear, and the sadness that sank in as they wheeled our mom out on a stretcher. We were surrounded by firefighters, police, and strangers who took my brothers and me away.

We were initially put in a home together, but even with my brothers nearby, I felt the absence of real connection. Our foster mom was cold and demanding. After several months, I was taken away from my brothers and moved into another foster home. The pain of losing my brothers was unbearable at the time. And yet, something happened that I never expected. In this new home, I experienced true kindness. Gentle words. Steady routines. Love, without strings attached.

At first, I didn't trust my new foster family. I'd built walls for a reason. But little by little, those walls came down.

I remember our Friday night roller skating trips, the sound of wheels on the hardwood floor, the fun '70s Disco music playing, and laughter that felt unforced. I remember sitting at the kitchen table with my foster family and realizing I didn't have to earn my place there.

And most of all, I remember my foster dad. The way he stayed calm when someone lost their temper. The way he made me feel seen and heard with no fear of what he would do to me. For the first time in my life, I felt truly safe. I wasn't pretending. I could be true to who I was. I could simply be a kid. I formed connections with this new family that supported my growth. And I began to see a vision for my future. One that included a loving, joyful family, where everyone felt safe.

When I was reunited with my mom and brothers, I felt two things at once—joy and heartbreak. I had longed for this moment, but it hurt to leave the family that allowed me to be a kid.

Once we were settled, I quickly became the twelve-year-old caretaker. My single mom was always gone, so I took on the responsibilities of the home and my brothers. But something unexpected lifted me again—a church bus that picked up kids in our apartment complex for Sunday School. That youth group became my second sanctuary. Surrounded by music, laughter, and families so different from mine, I saw new possibilities. I could laugh freely, sing loudly, and feel lighter.

That season gave me another chance to be true to myself. I built connections that helped me grow. Once again, my vision expanded. I saw the kind of life I wanted to create, and the kind of parent I hoped to become.

After high school, I joined the Air Force as a Security Police Specialist—a career choice dominated by men. The training was intense. I started off unsure and often overwhelmed, but I pushed through. I found my voice. I discovered what I was capable of. I could be true to who I was. I could be strong and soft, disciplined and intuitive.

With every base where I was assigned, from the U.S. to Germany, Turkey, and Saudi Arabia, I found community. The military teaches you how to show up for one another fast. We formed connections that helped each other grow. Finally, I saw myself as strong, not just in my role, but in who I was becoming.

The military gave me confidence, structure, and financial independence. But most of all, it showed me the power of being true to myself and deepened my vision for the future I wanted to create.

I later married and, together, we built our dream. I started Trofholz Technologies in 2001. My husband joined in 2002, and we poured everything into the business. We grew rapidly into an eight-figure business with over one hundred employees and fulfilled large-scale federal contracts.

At the same time, we raised four children. I managed to stay involved in all of their activities from school events and sports to volunteer roles. I led my business and showed up in my community. I networked with industry leaders. On the outside, it looked like we were the couple who had it all: a thriving business, a beautiful family, and a house full of achievement.

But no one saw how lonely I felt inside. How disconnected I was from myself again. I didn't feel emotionally safe or supported. I was performing, not living. I had lost myself in the very life I had worked so hard to build.

In the fall of 2015, everything crumbled.

I discovered a truth I had been avoiding for too long. For years, I had carried suspicions, quiet questions I tried to silence. Eventually, I learned the truth, and it shattered everything I thought I could count on. At first, I tried to pretend like everything was fine. I poured myself into work. My weight dropped to ninety-eight pounds. I went numb. But I couldn't keep hiding.

In December 2015, at our company year-end meeting, my husband and I stood in front of our team to share the news that we were separating. Tears welled up in our eyes. For the first time in our professional lives, we dropped the mask. He stood next to me and acknowledged he had made serious mistakes. Something shifted in that moment for me—I stopped pretending. I learned how powerful it was to be true to myself and others.

In 2016, I began rebuilding myself again. But this time, from the inside out.

I walked over mountains, along rivers, and beside the ocean. I reflected. I dove into self-discovery with the same focus I'd once used to scale a company. I devoured books and filled pages in my journal. I let myself grieve and release the shame I was carrying. It didn't happen all at once. Some days I felt hollow. Other days, hopeful. But I kept showing up. I kept asking the hard questions. I stopped making decisions to please others and began to trust my intuition.

I rebuilt relationships, starting with the one I had with myself. I surrounded myself with people who challenged me to be honest, not perfect. I began telling the truth of my story, not just the polished version. I stopped apologizing for wanting more.

In January 2020, I wrote a 10-year vision of who I wanted to *be* both personally and professionally. A vision rooted in clarity, connection, and purpose. That vision became my map, my filter, and my fuel.

The more I aligned with my vision and learned to set boundaries, the more my future naturally unfolded. In 2023, I opened The Rising Zone. It wasn't just another business I was creating. It was about answering a call to inspire others to rise through their storms, not in spite of them, but because of them.

My vision is still unfolding and I know there will always be storms in life. But now, when I feel myself starting to drift, I recognize it faster. I step outside. I breathe. I hold a rock in my hand, remind myself that I've weathered much worse, and reconnect with the calm inside of me. I return to the same three questions that have always carried me through:

- Am I being true to myself and others?
- Am I creating connections that support growth?
- Am I aligning with my vision?

These aren't just reflections. They're my compass—and my anchor.

About the Author:

Yvonne Pire is a USAF veteran, award-winning entrepreneur, and founder of Trofholz Technologies, one of the top woman-owned federal security integrators in the nation. After building an eight-figure business while raising four children, she experienced a personal breaking point in 2015 that sparked her deeper mission: to help high performers lead with purpose without sacrificing their wellbeing. In 2023, she founded *The Rising Zone*, a coworking wellness center and home to *RZ Connect*, a growing community redefining success through authenticity, resilience, and human connection.

Scan the QR Code to Learn More:

The story doesn't end here. It's just the beginning of yours. If Unshakeable stirred something within you, your truth, your strength, your hunger for alignment, then it's time to step into what's next. If you're ready to stop performing and start leading from within, join me by clicking above or scanning the QR code.

Interested in Becoming One of the Authors in an Upcoming Project?

Sharing your story isn't just an act of courage—it's a gift. The voices in this collection remind us that our experiences, when shared, can uplift, connect, and inspire others in ways we may never fully see. If you found hope, strength, or insight in these pages, know that your own story could do the same for someone else.

To learn more about contributing to a future volume, visit www.careyconley.com. We'd love to hear from you.

Unshakeable Endorsements

David Meltzer

Unshakeable is more than a book, it's a movement. Each story turns pain into power and offers a roadmap for facing life's storms with persistence and a deeper purpose.

— **David Meltzer**
Speaker | Author | Entrepreneur
Chairman, Napoleon Hill Institute

Rita Davenport

Resilience is not about avoiding hardship, but about rising through it. *Unshakeable* captures this truth with stories that inspire strength, courage, and hope in the face of life's adversities.

— **Rita Davenport, CSP, CPAE**
Speaker | Author | Business Leader
President of Arbonne International (1991–2011)

Wendy Aimee Porter

Each chapter in *Unshakeable* is unique, transparent, and deeply touching. The wide variety of stories makes this book so compelling, there's truly something here that will resonate with everyone, no matter their age or stage of life.

— **Wendy Aimee Porter**
Women's Empowerment and Business Mentor

Made in the USA
Coppell, TX
19 January 2026

66776174R00089